Praise for

MANTRAS IN MOTION

"When I was introduced to Erin's work, I discovered how to truly feel and embody my desires. Suddenly the link between my mind, body, and desires made perfect sense. As she always says, 'Movement in your body means movement in your life.' This book is for you if you're ready to move smoothly into a life you love."

— **Jessica Ortner**, *New York Times* best-selling author of *The Tapping Solution for Weight Loss and Body Confidence*

"Welcome to a revolution in mind-heart-body transformation. With a masterful combination of mindfulness and movement, heart and hustle, Mantras in Motion *will help you embody your best self from the inside out, radiating contagious joy from every fiber of your being. Erin's unique combination of powerful practices will get you moving, dancing, singing, and celebrating—elevating your entire life in the process."*

— **Jenny Blake**, author of *Pivot: The Only Move That Matters Is Your Next One*

"This book isn't just words on a page, it's energy injected into your life. This isn't just for reading, it's about experiencing how you want to feel, and how you want to show up, now. Get up and move, speak the words Erin gives you, and see your life and your body transform."

— **Alexandra Jamieson**, author of *Women, Food, and Desire* and co-author of *Getting to Hell Yes*

"Getting out of your head and into your heart is the key to creating positive and long-lasting change in your life. With an intoxicating mix of movement, mantras, and meditation, Erin will remind you that anything is possible with intention and inspiration. This incredibly refreshing approach to wellness will not only work out your body, it will also feed your soul."

— **Heather K. Jones**, dietitian and *New York Times* best-selling co-author of *The Skinnytaste Cookbook* and *Skinnytaste Fast and Slow*

"A must-read for anyone who wants to embrace and truly embody the power of positivity. Erin reminds us how we can feel good in our mind, body, and heart (all at once!) through movement and mantras."

— **Robyn Youkilis**, health coach, TV host, speaker, and author of *Thin from Within*

"I didn't realize I was intellectualizing the manifesting process rather than embodying it. Erin's methods have blown me away and I can feel a whole new level of manifesting magic flowing through me. A game changer!"

— **Denise Duffield-Thomas**, author of *Get Rich, Lucky Bitch!*

"I've spent endless hours in the gym, doing mindless reps, and running on treadmills to nowhere. And I've worked for decades on my spiritual health. I couldn't have imagined there was something I could do that would nourish my soul at the same time as supporting my physical fitness. Erin's methods in Mantras in Motion *deliver just that—a wellness practice for all of me (mind, body, and spirit)."*

— **Rebekah Borucki**, meditation guide and author of *You Have 4 Minutes to Change Your Life*

"As a hypnotherapist, I am always focused on making sure that transformation takes place in the location where it can have the greatest impact . . . in the subconscious mind. Erin has created a way to combine movement, motivation, and (in my mind) the most important piece, a way to bypass the critical thinking mind and transform the subconscious directly while having fun!"

— **Grace Smith**, celebrity hypnotherapist, founder of Grace Space Hypnosis, and author of *Close Your Eyes, Get Free*

"Mantras in Motion *is the perfect combination of thought and action! It's an inspiring read that made me feel excited to make real, meaningful changes in my life each day. Erin has a gift for making people feel limitless, and that comes through on every page."*

— **Caissie Levy**, Broadway actress and singer

"As a physician I have recommended Erin Stutland's work to countless patients and clients over the last decade. If I could have asked for one comprehensive resource, Mantras in Motion *is exactly what I would have wished for. It's the perfect companion to help you achieve any health or life goals that you may have."*

— **Dr. Samantha Brody**, naturopathic physician and author of *Overcoming Overwhelm*

"I have used the tools in this book to write plays and TV episodes I'm really proud of, and also to regularly remind myself that my brain, emotions, and body work really great together. Erin's book provides so many ways to open and bring a lot of movement and delight into the process, reminding us that we can love who we are right now, as well as welcome who we are becoming."

— **Kirsten Vangsness**, actor and playwright

MANTRAS IN MOTION

MANTRAS IN MOTION

MANIFESTING WHAT YOU WANT THROUGH MINDFUL MOVEMENT

ERIN **STUTLAND**

HAY HOUSE, INC.
Carlsbad, California • New York City
London • Sydney • New Delhi

Published in the United States by: Hay House, Inc.: www.hayhouse.com®
Published in Australia by: Hay House Australia Pty. Ltd.: www.hayhouse.com.au
Published in the United Kingdom by: Hay House UK, Ltd.: www.hayhouse.co.uk
Published in India by: Hay House Publishers India: www.hayhouse.co.in

Indexer: Jay Kreider • *Cover design:* Karla Baker • *Interior design:* Nick C. Welch
Interior illustrations: © Laura Baran

Cataloging-in-Publication Data is on file with the Library of Congress

Hardcover ISBN: 978-1-4019-5527-4
e-book ISBN: 978-1-4019-5528-1

10 9 8 7 6 5 4 3 2 1

1st edition, January 2019

Printed in the United States of America

For Lance and Kwynn—for you came,
and landed in my arms.
My cup runneth over.

CONTENTS

Dear Reader,

Here's to creating movement in your body and movement in your life!

A book will only have a lasting impact if you apply the wisdom it holds. To help you, I've created some resources to take your experience to the next level.

As this book's owner, you have exclusive access to **movement videos** so we can do them together, **guided audio meditations** so you can listen to them and relax, and **PDFs of mantras** to print so you have a visual reminder of your intentions.

You can get all these resources at www.erinstutland.com/gifts. I hope you'll find they help you with your practice.

Enjoy!

xx,
Erin

FOREWORD

Have you ever received a lifeline from a caring friend that ended up being exactly what you needed to get unstuck?

Years ago, I was feeling burnout and disconnected from both my creativity and my body. At the time, I was working on a book that was intended to help nourish and uplift people, yet I was totally running on empty.

That's when my friend, the brilliant and talented Erin Stutland, swooped in and kick-started a spiritual fitness practice that has fueled my life—and my success—for close to a decade now.

She must have picked up on my exhaustion during a catch-up chat, because the next day an email with one of her inspiring mantra-driven workouts was waiting in my inbox. I gratefully pressed play, got off my butt, and was completely amazed by the mental and physical transformation I experienced in just 15 minutes—I felt frickin' fantastic!

Not only did I want more of this feeling, but my body began to crave a new kind of movement that would strengthen both my muscles and my mindset. I'd been practicing meditation and affirmations for years, but I never thought to combine these powerful tools with fitness.

The way Erin combines movement with positive affirmations has the unique ability to rewire your brain, reset your mood, boost your energy, and get your creative mojo flowing. Plus, she's an absolute joy to learn from—she's positive and encouraging and just has this way of making you feel like you're getting sage advice from a dear friend

And how does the saying go? If you want movement in your life, you need movement in your body. Well, couple that with Erin's teachings and you will literally become unstoppable. If you're in a rut like I was at the time or if you're ready to uplevel your health, happiness, and abundance, this book holds the key to your success.

The positive shifts we all want to make start in our minds. Each of us has thousands of thoughts per day—many of which are negative! In fact, human beings are actually wired to be negative. It's part of our evolution and survival mechanism. But when we feed ourselves a steady diet of negativity, fear, and anxiety, it's nearly impossible to create the lives we desire, let alone the vibrant health we seek.

And here's the thing, feeling our very best is the goal, because the better we feel, the more likely we are to share our light (aka our unique magic), which is why we're here in the first place.

So if you want to change your life, go for your dreams, and embrace your fullest potential, you need to channel your energy in the best and brightest direction possible. This is where Erin comes in and why she's so genius. Erin's powerful work has inspired countless people to step into their strength and manifest their greatness. She's a spiritual alchemist who can help you embrace your true power and purpose—body, mind, and spirit.

Let this book be your gateway to your highest good. Erin is lovingly and fiercely here to offer you a new way, just like she offered me on that fateful day. You've got this!

— **Kris Carr**, *New York Times* best-selling author, cancer thriver, and wellness activist

CHAPTER 1

WHY COMBINE MOVEMENT WITH MANTRAS?

Have you ever read a self-help book and felt fired up about all the changes that'll happen in your life only to find that nothing really changes much, if at all? Have you ever felt stuck . . . maybe even for years? Or maybe you have taken two steps forward but three steps back. Did you feel like a failure because of it?

Me too! Time and again, I wanted to make changes, but my vision for my life stayed trapped inside my head.

Over and over, my clients have told me how hard they've tried to follow all the advice they've been given. They've written their affirmations, created their vision boards, chanted mantras, meditated, and on and on. Yet they continued to contend with self-doubt, perfectionism, procrastination, depression, anxiety, or all of the above. They still found it hard to stick up for themselves, take good care of their bodies, or allow their authentic selves to step out into the world. They struggled to figure out what they wanted, or they couldn't seem to create it in their lives, whether it was a job, love, or financial security.

I've come to understand that so many of our efforts don't create a lasting impact because they don't include all of who we are. The power and energy of these glorious bodies we were given haven't been used nearly enough. Writing down affirmations begins to change the mind. Chanting mantras powerfully engages the voice. Meditation reduces stress and improves concentration. When you roll the benefits of all these practices one full-body experience, you put a powerful mindset into motion.

We might be writing those affirmations or creating those vision boards on a regular basis. But when we do finally move our bodies—feeling good for taking care of our physical health—what do we think about? While we go for a walk, do we bring to mind the affirmations we wrote, or are we thinking about our shopping lists? If we go to an exercise class, are we focusing on what we want to create in our lives, or do we guilt ourselves about the calories from last night's dinner? While riding a bike, do we focus on clearing out negative beliefs, or are we thinking, *I wish I didn't hate my job so much*? Or worse, while we are trying to get into the present moment, do we look at the woman next to us in yoga class and think, *Why can't I be skinny like her?*

Those thoughts are actually our own personal hit parade of "mantras" that create negative programming in our minds, hearts, and bodies every day. This negativity gets in the way of all we want to create in life, whether it's building self-confidence or landing a fabulous new job. As we think these negative "mantras" while moving our bodies, we inadvertently align all our energy—the body, heart, and mind—toward the creation of exactly what we *don't* want. Yikes!

What if we did the opposite, harnessing all our energy toward creating the changes we *do* want in life by saying *positive* mantras while we move? Here's what happens: when you move your body while repeating mantras—speaking your desires out loud for letting go, feeling better, or getting what you want—manifesting is no longer a purely intellectual exercise or an occasional craft project. Instead, you express your passion through your voice *and* your body, putting every ounce of your energy in service of what you want. Your voice vibrates through your cells and your bones, turning you into a tuning fork for your desires. Your body's movements put an exclamation point on your heart's desires, sending the energy of what you envision through your bloodstream and your nervous system.

Movement in your body creates movement in your life. Movement with mantras supercharges both your movement and your ability to create the sweet life you want.

When you put positive mantras into motion, you accomplish four key goals:

- you plant uplifting thoughts in your mind so there is no room for negative ones, as these new, more empowered ideas take up all your mental space;
- you get out of your head and more connected to your body, helping you to stay in the present moment and out of doubt and fear;
- you use your body and your voice to put every ounce of energy you have toward creating your best life; and
- you feel good in your mind *and* heart *and* body because you're taking care of *all of you* at once.

This trifold approach will increase your positive energy, further fueling your passion for what you want and reinforcing your belief that you can have what you most desire! Your intentions—whether tangible like finding a romantic partner or more internal like learning how to say no—will pulsate through you and become part of you. The movement makes the words more potent, and the words make the movement more potent. Talk about feeling fired up!

This is why *Mantras in Motion* is the next generation of mind-heart-body transformation. It's 360 degrees, no longer separating your body from the rest of who you are. It's what has worked best for me, and I'm confident it will work for you too.

But let me be clear about an important point: *this is not a fitness or workout book*. It isn't about rigorous physical exercise. You can reap the benefits even with easy movements. I'm going to teach you some very simple moves in each chapter that you'll use along with the mantras to change your life. Rest assured:

this is a life-transformation book that uses the power of movement to make that transformation happen. The steps I'll walk you through are easy and fun, and they're meant to help you solve issues, as well as create a better life—whatever that means to you.

I can't wait to tell you more about this transformational plan that has made such a difference for me and so many others, but before I do, let me tell you about my own journey that led me to this mantras-and-movement method.

My Story

I grew up as a dancer. You may think being a dancer must be fabulous, but let me tell you—it's a lot of pressure to feel like you always have to be skinny and perfect!

I looked at the other dancers—some of them were tall and *really* skinny with legs for days. I, on the other hand, was just 5'4" and starting to get curves. I thought I was supposed to look like those other girls, so I monitored everything I put in my mouth and obsessed over it. What I didn't know is that when you don't eat, your anxiety and obsessive behavior only get worse.

My need for perfection escalated when I went off to earn a dance degree in college. It was strange to be graded on my every move. The joy was sapped right out of me, and suddenly, dancing became only about becoming a better dancer. I began to believe that whatever I did and how I did it was never enough. I believed *I* wasn't enough.

As I continued through that first semester, I began to feel really "off." It got harder and harder to drag myself to dance class each day. I didn't feel like socializing, and in my down time, all I wanted to do was sleep.

Then I came across a magazine article about depression. It listed the symptoms, and I was shocked to recognize myself. Really? I was depressed? How did this happen? Keep in mind, this was before there were hundreds of drug commercials on TV offering up a solution for depression. It wasn't talked about that much, so the stigma was even more widespread than it is today.

After reading that article, I still felt alone, but I was relieved to find out there was a name for what I was experiencing and perhaps even some help for it. But before I could do anything about my depression, I received news that dwarfed everything. My mother was diagnosed with ovarian cancer.

It further shook every foundation I had managed to build in my young life. The idea that I could possibly lose my mom before I was 20 made me feel helpless and out of control.

Even so, there was an amazing aspect to the experience. Mom had always believed in the mind-body connection, so while she had chemotherapy and a hysterectomy like her Western doctors advised, she also found a wonderful cancer wellness center where they taught meditation, tai chi, and nutrition.

When I was home from school, I watched my mother in awe. She wasn't about to let her illness stop her. Every day, she put on her cute little hat to cover her bald head, went out into the world, and made the most of whatever energy she had. The power of her fierce attitude inspired me and taught me a lot about how to be in the world. She has been a profound role model for me since day one, but her courage throughout this challenge turned her into superwoman in my eyes. And I'm happy to report that all these years later, my mom is here and doing great!

Thanks to her, I became aware of how much power my mind and attitude have over my ability to heal, and I was determined to make a change for the better. Using my mom's example as inspiration to heal my depression, I started seeing a therapist and attending a local yoga class.

The yoga class on campus was taught by an old man with a long white beard. I instantly loved the spiritual aspect of yoga in which moving the body teaches devotion, intention, and connection with the divine, even if yoga was a bit of a "no-no" among dancers at the time. I still loved dance, but it included a lot of pressure. Yoga was movement with an entirely new dimension that didn't just feel good to my body but also nurtured my soul. And my poses didn't have to be perfect!

Then, during a visit home from school one weekend, I came across a book in my parents' basement. It was called *The Greatest Salesman in the World*, by Og Mandino. Now, I wasn't planning to go into sales, but this book contained daily readings filled with lessons on success in life, not just sales. Each lesson was to be read three times a day and contained affirmations or positive phrases that immediately attracted my attention. And while I didn't sell anything, I did start to feel a whole lot better just by virtue of thinking more positive thoughts. I didn't yet know how to use my body to help me reinforce those positive thoughts and manifest what I wanted, but Mandino's book planted an important seed in me.

Changing the Channel

Over the next several years, I used affirmations more and more, and I continued my yoga and meditation practices. But it wasn't until a few years into my spiritual development that I had a *big* epiphany.

I had made the transition from dance into acting and was living in New York City, auditioning for film and television. One day, I had a callback audition for a new television show that was a big-deal opportunity. Do you know what it feels like when you're in the groove and you can just tell you've nailed an interview or pitch? Well . . . this wasn't one of those times.

When I arrived at the audition, there was so much at stake that my nerves got the better of me. I couldn't connect with the character, I fumbled my lines, and I felt self-conscious when the casting director looked at me. I walked out knowing I hadn't gotten the job. *You really screwed that up, Erin*, I thought.

I was disappointed in myself—ashamed even. But I was supposed to meet friends for the weekend, so I got on the train and promptly started obsessing over everything I'd done wrong in the audition. There was a part of me that truly believed if I obsessed about it enough, I could figure out how to do better in my next audition. But as I sat there telling myself how awful I was, another voice penetrated the gloom. "You're beating yourself up. You always do this—obsess about your mistakes until you feel worse. And has it ever really helped you solve a problem?" I couldn't remember one time when my obsessing actually improved anything. Instead, I'd stay stuck in a never-ending loop of negativity.

Einstein has been credited as saying, "No problem can be solved from the same level of consciousness that created it." So I thought, *You're going to spend the weekend with great friends in a wonderful house on the beach. Do you* really *want to feel like crap the whole time? Do you truly want to obsess about this audition the entire weekend like you usually do?* The answer was a resounding no!

What if I just thought about something else? It sounded so simple. Could I just "change the channel" and switch my thoughts? Well, it was worth a try. So I started searching my mind for a subject to focus on that might help me feel good. Building a new website seemed like a good topic. I was excited about it, and I could visualize how I wanted it to look, experimenting with different configurations in my head. Almost immediately, I felt lighter and more at ease.

Even so, my mind tried to pull me back to the audition. So I continually coaxed it back to the website or what I was looking forward to during my weekend. In no time, I'd be seeing one of my best girlfriends, smelling the ocean (one of my favorite scents), and falling asleep to the sound of the waves. I had so much to look forward to and occupy my mind, but those negative thoughts wouldn't let up.

It was like babysitting a child who keeps hitting his brother and won't stop. I started to talk to that negative part of myself like a stern yet loving parent. "That's not how we act. You're not being nice, and you need to have a time-out until you're ready to behave." Every time that negative voice would come back, I would put on that parental "hat." *You're being mean. You're not being nice. I'm not going to discuss the audition with you right now.*

I had to say this several times to myself before I made it to my destination. But by the time I got off the train, I felt calmer and less emotionally charged by the audition experience.

It was a tangible lesson in how obsessing over mistakes does nothing to bring insights or peace and how switching the channel can make a huge difference in how you feel. I knew it would take work to change the channel on a regular basis, but after that experience, it was clear the results would be well worth the effort.

Even more importantly, I finally understood that I had the power to change the way I speak *to* myself and *about* myself every day. And yet I wanted more. I didn't just want to change my thoughts. I wanted to change my life.

Around this time, I found a wonderful mentor named Patricia Moreno, who was combining fitness with positive affirmations. It was a beautiful marriage of my passions for positive thinking and movement, and I finally started to become unstuck from my past habits.

After working closely with Patricia, I began to develop my own process that combined dance, yoga, coaching, meditation, and transformation. This method became my workout class called Shrink Session.

Indeed, *Shrink Session* is a double entendre. You're not only shrinking your waistline; you're shrinking your doubts, fears, and obstacles to happiness—the same way you might if you went to see a "shrink." (While I don't normally use that word for psychiatrists, it was too perfect to resist for the name of my class.)

The majority of people came to my Shrink Sessions because they wanted to create a change in their bodies. But they walked away with so much more. Time and again, they found that using the mantras with movement brought returns in different areas of their lives beyond their body and their expectations—all from a workout class. I've watched them land dream jobs on the Broadway stage, find soulful relationships that result in marriage, conceive a child after trying for a long time, find their spark again after a devastating loss, and, of course, build a sustainable, loving relationship with their bodies. It's the whole enchilada, baby!

Today, I can't imagine moving without mantras. The combo of movement and mantras heightens my ability to design the sweetest possible life. It's like the difference between a Hyundai and a Ferrari. Why wouldn't I want to add that power to my creative engine?

Is This Book Right for You?

If you've ever wanted to change your life for the better, this book is for you. It's that simple. As you read these pages, you'll begin to understand the immense responsibility you play in your own happiness, recognizing your own power in co-creating your reality and your future.

Before you can reap the benefits of moving with the mantras, however, you'll need to tackle some of your issues and get to know yourself on a deeper level. So each chapter will include topics for you to consider, meditations for you to do, and journaling exercises for you to write. It *is* a book, so you'll primarily engage your mind and heart until you get to the movement with mantras portion of each chapter. That's where the power will get ramped up so that you can take what you've learned and make it a fountain of positive energy! This final part of the process will solidify your intentions for what you want to change in your life.

Each chapter will include:

- stories from my life or my clients' lives (with their names changed in most cases to protect their privacy);
- a meditation or visualization, which you can do using the written version or the audio version on my website;
- journaling exercises to engage your mind and turn negative thoughts to positive;
- a fun, rhythmic mantra to make your intentions solid, strong, and vibrant; and
- easy movements that you can do while you repeat the mantras.

Each mantra will be repeated throughout the chapter so that it becomes indelible in your mind and a part of your heart as you meditate. Then you'll make the mantra a part of your body when you combine it with the movements. Once you engage all parts of you toward your goal, you'll be on your way to custom designing your life!

At the end of the book, I'll provide you with a 14-day plan so you can design that life using the power of the two M's—movement and mantras.

How to Use This Book

You can read the chapters from start to finish, or you can jump around to the issues you want to work on the most. That said, I do ask that you complete the first journaling exercise about core values before you move on to other chapters because you'll use it as you complete other exercises throughout the book.

Regardless of the order you read the chapters, you can always come back to certain chapters later as your priorities change and use the mantras that are most relevant to your current circumstances. *Use the book in the way that best works for you!*

Here are answers to some of the questions you might have about how to complete the movements and mantras:

Do I have to say the mantras out loud during the movements?

Yes, please! While you perform my specific movements, saying the mantras out loud creates a sound vibration throughout your body that becomes a lightning rod for what you want. You might feel awkward at first, but to make changes in your life, you have to step out of your comfort zone. Plus, you never know what positive effect you might have on your family. If your kids or partner hear you chanting your mantras, they'll learn positive self-talk from your example. One of my clients' husbands says he feels proud and inspired when he hears his wife saying her mantras while she exercises.

Can I use the mantras with my own movement practice or in a class?

Of course! I invite you to incorporate these mantras into your life whenever and however you can. I designed these particular movements so that it would be easy to coordinate the moves and mantras together. Therefore, if you start by following the plan, it will help you learn how these two powerful forces can come together. That being said, the beauty of these mantras is that you can also use them with any type of movement, whether kickboxing, martial arts, yoga, power walking, or any kind of chair exercise you like to do. The more you say the mantras while you move in any way, the faster you'll design the life you choose.

How challenging are the movement sections?

I've made them simple on purpose so that you can easily say the mantras with the movements. If you find them difficult at any point, decrease your range of motion or modify the movement so that it feels good for you. It is more important to stay in motion than anything else. Through repetition, you will find that the patterns will get easier each time.

With that, try to do these moves wtih as much precision as possible. Act as if you were born to do this! When we're sloppy with our movements, we send a message to our mind, heart, and body that we aren't committed to what we're doing. I know that isn't true. Otherwise, you wouldn't be reading this book! But notice how I say *precision* and not *perfection*. You're simply going for steady progress. Each time you commit to doing your best, your best only gets better. And your best is always good enough.

As you move, allow your breath to soothe you, as well as your body. I call it "staying easy."

If you find yourself feeling challenged, notice where your mind wants to go. Does it rush to blame, worry, fear, or doubt? Pay attention, and gently bring your thoughts back to the mantras.

Do you have videos that I can watch to make sure I do the movements correctly?

Yes! I have created a few videos of the movements to help you. You can access them at www.erinstutland.com/gifts.

How long will the movement portions of the chapters take?

Each movement section takes just five minutes! I want you to see that you don't have to work out hard or for a long time to reap the benefits of movement with mantras. In just five minutes, you can achieve a mental and emotional shift while also achieving improved physical fitness.

Now, I know it's all fine and good to say that the movement sections will only take five minutes, but you might be tempted to pass by those sections and start reading the next chapter, thinking, *These are great, Erin, but I'll do them later.* In fact, I asked my friend Claire to test the moves for me, but when I checked in with her at the end of the day, she said, "Shoot, Erin! I didn't get to it. And tomorrow is really busy for me. Then, this weekend, I have to take my daughter to a birthday party."

I stopped her and said with a chuckle, "Claire, it's literally five minutes! If you can't give yourself the gift of five minutes a day to focus on you and what you really want in your life, how are you ever going to create it?" She got my point and went off right away to try the moves and mantras.

She texted me immediately after: "Wow, Erin! I feel so much better! I'm amazed that five minutes can shift my mood and thinking that much."

So please don't skip these sections in each chapter. They're what will bring all your other work in the chapters together and help you make that sweet life you want a reality.

Do I need a lot of space to do these movements?

Not at all! You'll only need the amount of space your body takes up when in a lunge position.

Do I need to wear special clothes or shoes, or have equipment?

No. Whatever you like is fine as long as you're comfortable. Some people like to move while barefoot. Others prefer sneakers. (A yoga mat might be helpful, however, if you're barefoot.)

How do the movements work?

You will learn two new moves in each chapter. They're simple enough that you should be able to focus on the mantras at the same time. They're also energizing enough that you'll get a mental, emotional, and physical boost!

Each mantra in the book consists of four lines like a short poem. Here's an example:

I let the desire guide me (line 1)
I have faith in its voice (line 2)
It leads me to my truth (line 3)
It clarifies my choice (line 4)

You'll perform Move 1 with Line 1 for 16 reps. (A rep means you perform the whole movement from beginning to end.) Then you'll perform Move 2 with Line 2 for 16 reps. You'll repeat Move 1 with Line 3 for 16 reps, followed by Move 2 again with Line 4 for 16 reps. I've done it this way so that you only have to perform two moves in each chapter, even though each mantra consists of four lines.

Here is an example of how it will look:
Move 1 with Line 1 for 16 reps
Move 2 with Line 2 for 16 reps
Move 1 with Line 3 for 16 reps
Move 2 with Line 4 for 16 reps

Next, you'll chant each line of the mantra in succession—lines 1 through 4—as you do the moves. Here's what I mean:

Move 1 with Line 1 for 1 rep
Move 2 with Line 2 for 1 rep
Move 1 with Line 3 for 1 rep
Move 2 with Line 4 for 1 rep

You'll then repeat that 4-move/4-line sequence ten times. Don't worry—it will be laid out clearly for you in each chapter.

Is there a way to print out the mantras in large print?

Yes, I've taken care of that for you too! Each mantra is a downloadable PDF on my website that you can print. Simply visit this link: www.erinstutland.com/gifts.

How can I count reps while saying the mantras out loud?

When you perform the moves, I suggest you say the mantra followed by the rep number in a whisper. For example, you'd say, "I let the desire guide me" in full voice, followed by "one" (or whichever rep number you're on) in a whisper.

What if I don't believe the mantras while I say them?

When you say a mantra that's opposed to the negative thoughts you've held your whole life, it's natural to have trouble believing them at first. That's one of the reasons why I invite you to vary how you say the mantras. You might want to say them loudly with a lot of gusto, or you may prefer to say them softly with sweetness directed toward yourself. Make it a game, and don't give up. The more you say the mantras, the more you'll start to believe them.

What if I get emotional while I say the mantras?

This happens for some people because it has been so long since they have spoken kindly to themselves.

The emotion is a release of the negativity and fear you've been holding on to, so it's a good sign! Don't be afraid of the feelings. Where there's emotion, there's often motion! This means that your inner world is moving, changing, and shaking up. That's exactly what you want in order to create a sweeter life. So just keep going, and let yourself feel whatever comes to the surface. If you need to stop for a few minutes and have a hard cry, do it. You'll feel a sense of relief after. (Of course, if intense emotions come up and don't resolve soon after you've finished performing the moves and mantras, please see a therapist to help you work through your feelings.)

Should I use music with the movements and mantras?

This is strictly up to you, but I find that music makes the exercises and mantras more fun and can evoke powerful emotions that add to the energy you're working to create. I love to create Spotify playlists for different moods to use while I exercise with mantras. Feel free to find me there or to create some of your own.

Can I create mantras of my own to do with movement?

Absolutely! Feel free to be as creative as you like. Just make sure your mantras are about what you *want* rather than what you *don't* want. Keep them positive and in the present tense! For example: instead of saying, "Every day, I let go of my negativity," you'd say, "Every day in every way, I am more positive."

Can I do the mantras and movements with my family or friends?

Of course! Chanting mantras together while you move puts even more energy toward what you're working to change or create, especially since it's more fun than doing it alone.

Are you fired up yet? If you've gotten this far already, it means you have the drive and willingness to make a change. That alone is huge.

I'll be right here alongside you, cheering you on as you move your body, open your heart, expand your mind, and manifest your dreams.

One of my favorite Martin Luther King, Jr., quotes is "Faith is taking the first step, even when you don't see the whole staircase." So that's what I'm going to encourage you to do. Just take this one page at a time, one action at a time. Before you know it, your beautiful mind, heart, and body will be filled with new thoughts, feelings, and ideas. You might not even recognize yourself!

What if I'm limited in the amount of movement I can do?

If you are limited in the amount of movement you can do, I encourage you to create movements to accommodate your body. Even if that means sitting in a chair and only doing upper body movement, that's okay! (Just be sure to incorporate the mantras!)

Along those lines, I have done my best to make this book as inclusive as possible, so that no matter your age, background, race, gender, or sexual preference, you can apply these tools to create a more satisfying life. Manifesting can be a tricky subject today. While the world would like us to believe that we all arrive on this earth on an equal playing field, I acknowledge that there are systems and biases in place that do not make that a reality. As a cis-gendered, white woman, I have socialized biases that I work hard to dismantle. I would also like to be a part of transforming the systems that put those biases in place. If I have missed the mark in any way or seem exclusionary, please don't hesitate to reach out. I am here to do my very best and am always striving to do better. As I learn and grow, I love learning from you too.

Make It Fun!

A fun way to remember your mantras while you move is to put on your artist hat, print out the mantra and some of your favorite images, and place them on the wall in the room where you do the movements. Remember, you can print PDF downloads of each chapter's mantra here: www.erinstutland.com/gifts. If you like, get creative and make your own mantra art! Be sure to share it on social media! Please pop by my Facebook page at https://www.facebook.com/EStutland/ or Instagram @erin.stutland using the hashtag #mantrasinmotion. Be sure to tag me so that I can be inspired by YOU!

UNEARTH YOUR DESIRES

Maybe I just don't know how to be satisfied. Maybe what I want is a fairy tale.

Those thoughts felt awful, but my mind kept at me. *I'm too hard to please. I want too much. Maybe this is as good as it gets.*

The problem was that what I had wasn't bad *at all*. I was in a relationship with a truly great guy. He was good to me, and we had a lot of fun together. If I held him up next to the list of traits of the perfect man for me, I'd check yes by all the boxes. But I still had that nagging feeling . . .

Sigh. *So shut up already, Erin.*

But I just couldn't shake the feeling that something wasn't quite right. Wasn't I supposed to feel "lit up" by my relationship? Or does that only happen in the movies?

One day, I met a therapist at a gathering, and I expressed my feelings of uncertainty about my boyfriend. "You know, Erin," she said, "the relationship doesn't have to be a fairy tale for it to work. You aren't going to feel madly in love every day."

Was that my reality check? I left the conversation feeling confused and sad. I wasn't expecting an "every moment is perfect" kind of relationship as she seemed to think. There was just something missing that I couldn't put my finger on. But I was scared. I thought I'd be a fool to throw away such a wonderful person. Plus, the idea that I was getting too old and this was possibly my last shot at finding love hung over me daily.

So I kept pushing down that nagging, gnawing feeling that something wasn't right. And every time I denied that feeling, I distanced myself from what I really wanted. I was desperately afraid that my true desires were a fantasy, not a possibility.

Then, a couple of months later, there was a tall, handsome guy in one of my NYC fitness classes. He came up to me after class to reintroduce himself. I say reintroduce because we had gone to elementary school together in Chicago. We chatted for a bit, said our goodbyes, and I didn't think much of it.

A few months later, I was still in my relationship, but it was becoming clearer why I'd had that nagging feeling. On a rainy afternoon, I was meeting with a friend who was visiting from out of state. She invited me to come over to the apartment that she was renting while in town. When I got to the lobby, lo and behold, there he was—that same handsome, tall fella from elementary school. He just happened to live in the building where my friend was staying. What are the odds? This time, I instantly felt excitement and an undeniable spark. But hey, I didn't *really* know him! And of course, I wasn't *really* available. Should I act on this feeling? How could I be sure if that feeling would be lasting? We've all had those immediate attractions that run their course before we know it, haven't we? *You're not available, Erin. Just stop it,* I told myself.

I knew, however, that following my feelings on this was important, even if it took me down an unknown path. So I reached out to him shortly after that run-in and suggested we get together, since we had so many friends and old experiences in common.

When we finally sat down to catch up over a glass of wine, I had a moment of total clarity. I saw the whole thing unfold before my eyes. I knew I was in the wrong relationship and that *this* was my guy. But, what should I do? I was still in this other relationship. I wanted to be respectful of that, but more so, even with this strong feeling I had, I still didn't trust it enough! I thought I should stick to the course I'd set for myself. I rationalized the feeling and chalked it up to a mere desire for distraction.

When we got together a second time, I was truthful with him about being in a relationship with someone and said it would be best if we were friends. I could tell he was disappointed, but he agreed. So this old friend and I began to develop a *new* friendship, and before I was even aware of it, I was falling in love with him.

Even though it was hard to come to terms with it, I realized that I'd found exactly what I'd been missing in my current relationship. If I wanted to live a life I was excited about and have a relationship that thrilled me, I was going to have to take the risk and listen to my heart. So I gathered up the courage to bring that other relationship to an end. I knew I wanted more, and I wasn't willing to settle.

What happened? That new old friend is now my husband. He is the absolute love of my life. And I came so close to never allowing myself to even get to know him!

My husband teases me about it now. "It took you *seven months* to break up with that other guy even though you knew you were in love with me!"

Yes, it took me that long. Why? Because I didn't trust what I wanted. And I know very well I'm hardly alone in that kind of distrust. I hear it and see it from the people in my classes and on my social media pages . . . *All. The. Time.*

We're so afraid to trust our true desires. We want guarantees. We want to know that everything will turn out perfectly. So we cut ourselves off from our desires—even our everyday little wants—before we even give them a chance. And when we do that, we cheat ourselves of all the possibilities the world sets at our feet.

If life is about anything, it's about embracing all of these possibilities. So let's tackle this desire head-on. You'll unearth your true desires, give yourself *permission* to want, and work with mantras and movement to create those desires. Movement in your life—that's what we're after!

Before you "move" on to your first journaling exercise, which will help you get clearer about your desires, I want to share the mantra you're going to internalize and vocalize throughout the chapter. This mantra is all about trusting your inner desire and the choices you make. I've added "I keep love in sight" because love is the most powerful fuel for making your desires a reality.

Are you ready? Repeat after me:

I let my desire guide me
I do what feels right
I stay true to my vision
I keep love in sight!

Let that sink in a little. You don't have to know your vision or believe the words of the mantra yet. But let's repeat it together one more time for good measure:

I let my desire guide me
I do what feels right
I stay true to my vision
I keep love in sight!

Journaling Exercise #1: Use Your Core Values as Your GPS

To kick-start your exploration, let's try our first journaling exercise. When you do any of the writing exercises and meditations in this book, please try to carve out a little quiet space for yourself, even if it's only for a few minutes. Maybe you'd like to curl up with a cup of tea, play some soft music, light a candle, or sit somewhere in nature. Do whatever works to help you concentrate. This is *your time.*

You'll also want to write down your answers because I'll sometimes ask you to refer back to them later. (You'll probably want to refer back to them too.) Feel free to write them on paper, in a notebook, or on your phone, tablet, or computer.

This first journaling exercise is the foundation of your desire. If you can gain clarity on your core values, the knowledge will help you decide exactly what you want. You'll know who you really are and what matters most to you.

I remember exactly when I realized that one of my core values was dancing. That may not sound like a typical core value, but to me, it wasn't just about dancing in a studio. It was about dancing through life. It was so important for me to feel rhythm in my body as I moved through my day. When I felt I had the freedom to move my body the way I wanted, even if I was sitting at my computer doing work, I felt more alive. This also meant that I needed to be in clothes and shoes that allowed me to move freely at any moment. Stiff shirts, pants with no stretch, and tight shoes made me feel depressed. When I identified this core value, it helped determine the environment I wanted and the clothes I wanted to wear!

Knowing your core values helps you separate the wheat from the chaff. You won't run the risk of thinking something is going to bring you fulfillment, only to work hard for it and find out it doesn't give you what you wanted after all.

1. Give yourself 15 minutes to do this exercise. Don't overthink it. You're not going for perfection; you're going for completion.
2. Read through the words in the following list, which represent a variety of values. Then write down the five that are most important to you. It might be difficult to choose just five, so take your time to determine the ones that truly matter the most. But the list is just to give you ideas! If you think of a value that isn't on the chart, feel free to add it. For instance, I added "dancing" to mine.

Abundance
Achievement
Accomplishment
Adventure
Affluence
Altruism
Appreciation
Autonomy
Beauty
Clarity
Collaboration
Commitment
Communication
Community
Connection to Others
Creativity
Emotional Health
Environment
Excellence
Family
Flexibility
Freedom
Friendship
Fulfillment
Fun
Healthy Living
Honesty
Humor
Inspiration
Integrity
Intimacy
Intuition
Joy
Kindness
Leadership
Loyalty
Partnerships
Personal Growth
Physical Appearance
Physical Fitness
Privacy
Professionalism
Promotions
Recognition
Respect
Risk-Taking
Romance
Security
Self-Actualization
Self-Care
Self-Expression
Self-Love
Self-Mastery
Sensuality
Service
Sharing
Spirituality
Status
Success
Trust
Truth
Vitality
Walking the Talk

3. Now let's go deeper. Take your list of values, and ask yourself, "What do I *mean* when I say that?" For example, if "kindness" is one of your values, what does kindness mean to you?

—No meanies?
—Gentle force in the world?
—Do no harm?

If "healthy living" is a value of yours, what does it mean to you?

—Feeling vibrant and alive?
—Loving your body?
—Eating a vegetarian diet?
—Being hot on the inside and out?
—Being a kick-ass, rock-star triathlete?

For each of your five most important values, write down what they mean to you.

4. Think about how these core values play out in your life. If you look at your behaviors and the experiences you choose, where do you honor these values? Are there areas where you *don't* honor them? Tell at least one good friend the five main core values you've pinpointed, and ask that friend to think of more examples of how you use these values in your life. What has your friend seen in you that shows these values?
5. Reflect on what you discovered about yourself and hold on to this list, as you'll refer to it again during other journaling exercises. Plus, it's helpful to look at it whenever you struggle with a decision. My husband teases me that I'm not a good decision-maker. Sometimes I get stuck because I want to make the "perfect decision." When I refer back to what's really truly important to me, though, the right choice becomes clearer. Always ask yourself: "Which of my choices are most in keeping with my core values?"

Inner vs. Outer Desires

We tend to think of desire only in terms of "stuff." But many of my clients and friends have described to me what I call "inner" desires rather than "outer" ones. An inner desire is a strength or quality you want to cultivate on the inside. An outer desire is an object or an experience, such as a car, vacation, job, or relationship.

My friend Diane says she's already managed to cultivate a lot of confidence in her life but is more easily derailed than she'd like. So one of her inner desires is to strengthen her self-confidence in order to stop worrying as much when she doesn't perform or behave perfectly in her work or personal life.

Some of the other inner desires that my clients have had include learning how to stick up for themselves, accepting themselves as they are, or becoming more comfortable with presenting their talents in the world.

Too often, we think of our inner issues as problems to solve rather than desires to fulfill. If we reframe them as qualities to "call in" and cultivate, they feel more within our power to create. For example, rather than thinking of a lack of self-confidence as an issue to fix, think of it as a strength to build within yourself.

Stretch Your "Want Muscle"

Even if you know your core values, you might hold yourself back from some of what you want. Many of us don't give ourselves permission to want more. We cut corners, skimp, choose the "lesser" one, the cheaper one, or the worse one.

Are there times you won't even admit what you want because you think it doesn't make rational sense? Like when you want something for no reason except that it would feel good or be fun? Do you walk away from the right partner like I almost did?

We're so worried that we'll be called indulgent, needy, slutty, or grandiose that we don't allow our lives to improve and expand as we could. We think our desires make us weak. How dare you want to make a lot of money! *You're greedy; shame on you!* How dare you want to be the star of the show! *Tsk-tsk, you're starved for attention.* How dare you want to just get laid? *Ooooh, you little slut!* How dare you want to eat that high-calorie scone? *Baaad. So, so bad.*

One of the reasons we deny our wants is that we think it's simply wrong to want. But I believe desire is naturally human. Even monks desire to be better at meditating!

We don't have to go to extremes and become heartless greed machines or materialistic, conspicuous consumers. If you ever tell yourself that what you want is "too much," ask yourself, *Who says?* After all, "too much" is just an arbitrary judgment. What would happen if you let that judgment go?

Maybe you tell yourself that what you want isn't possible. If that's your MO, remind yourself of something you've received that you never thought you'd have. I'll bet if you think about it, you've had at least two or three experiences like that in your life.

Here's an example from my life: when I was a kid studying dance, I devoured the TV show *Fame*. No one else in my family was a dancer, and we didn't know a soul in New York City. But I wanted so much to dance in a New York studio like the people I watched on *Fame*. I'd moon about it in front of the TV, but at the time, I didn't think it was at all possible.

Then one summer, I got the opportunity to go to New York, and before I knew it, I was dancing in several studios like the one on *Fame*. It was 100 percent possible!

One of my friends told me that when she was a child, she loved to watch nature programs set in Africa, Australia, Asia, and South America. Her parents were very fearful of the natural world, so it never even dawned on her that she could travel to such places and visit the very areas she'd watched on those shows. When she reached adulthood, though, that's exactly what she did. She's been to each of those continents, and she has loved every minute of it.

It makes me think of a quote I love from the late actress Audrey Hepburn. She started her life as a malnourished little girl during World War II who received aid from UNICEF and later became a Goodwill Ambassador for that same organization. She said, "Nothing is impossible. The word itself says, 'I'm possible!'"

Is there a dream that's been knocking on your door that you haven't dared to imagine could come true? Let's stretch your "want muscle."

Journaling Exercise #2: Dig for Gold and Set Your Vision

In this exercise, you will dig for gold to unearth the beautiful, shiny desires that live beneath the surface—even the stuff you're scared to admit.

1. Set a timer for 10 minutes to create a big mama jama *I want . . .* list. Start each line with *I want . . .* Try to

get your rational mind out of the driver's seat, give yourself permission to push beyond your edges, and be outrageous with your desires. Perhaps your desires include: I want to live in Paris for six months, build a dream house by the ocean, or start a business helping underprivileged youth. What you actually accomplish is unimportant; you're just stretching your "want muscles" and increasing your range.

2. Set your timer for another 10 minutes to create a second *I want . . .* list. This time, think about what you can do, achieve, have, or become during the next 12 months. Possible you might list: *I want to start dating again, blog regularly,* or *feel confident in my body.* (It's fine to repeat some of your desires from the first list.) The "how" isn't important right now, so stop yourself if you think, *This will never happen in the next year.* Sweetly say to that negative voice, "I see that you want my attention, but we'll have to discuss it later."
3. By each item, write how you want to *feel* since what you really want are the feelings you believe a desire will bring you. More money, for example, might make you feel secure, abundant, and free.
4. On your list for the next year, circle the three most important desires and the three most important feelings.
5. Write your top three desires and feelings in the present tense as if they already exist. For example: *I want to redecorate my living room* would become *My living room is beautifully redecorated, and I feel at home and inspired there*. Be sure to hold on to your lists because you'll refer back to them in later chapters.

Before we move on, let's revisit our mantra for this chapter:

I let my desire guide me
I do what feels right
I stay true to my vision
I keep love in sight!

It's All about the Feelings

When I was auditioning regularly as an actor, I attended acting class to keep my artistic muscles in shape. But once my business took off, I no longer had a desire to hone my craft. So I stopped taking classes. Fast forward to a few years into running my business, and I started hearing a gentle knock on my soul's door. It said, "Maybe you should go back to acting class." I quickly brushed it off because it didn't make sense. I wasn't looking to be cast in a Broadway show or a film. How could I make time for something so impractical?

But when a desire knocks on your soul's door, you need to listen, or it'll just start knocking louder and louder. As my knock increased in volume, I began to tune in to why it was suggesting I go back to acting class. It was a desire for truth telling.

More than anything, it's important to me to tell the truth about my feelings—even the not-so-pretty ones like anger, jealousy, insecurity, or fear. Acting class had always given me a safe environment to express and experience my true and sometimes "out there" feelings. Going back to class wasn't so impractical after all.

The point is that no matter what you desire—whether it's an inner quality or a new dress—it's all about what you believe you'll feel when you get it. My client Carrie admitted that she was jealous of a woman who had close to 200,000 Instagram followers and traveled the world talking about spirituality. She couldn't wrap her head around how this woman managed to get such a "lucky" job. It seemed as if the woman didn't care what people thought about her and just went after whatever she wanted.

When we dug a little deeper, it wasn't that Carrie wanted more Instagram followers or even to travel the world. It turns out that one of her core values was freedom, and that's what she really desired. She wanted to not care about what people thought of her. She wanted to feel that she could speak her mind and still be valued for her beliefs. Once we uncovered what she wanted to *feel,* we began working on the *form* that her sense of freedom would take in her life. And that form didn't look anything like the life of the woman that Carrie envied.

What if what you want is a new dress or suit? Let's say you see the perfect outfit in a store window, and you want it *bad.* Except it costs $400, which is way over your budget. There's absolutely nothing wrong with wanting that outfit, but it really isn't about the garment, is it? It's about what it will help you *feel.* Maybe you'll feel powerful, attractive, or sexy when you wear it. There's nothing wrong with wanting to feel any of that. But if you absolutely can't afford the clothing, you might be able to get those feelings through some other means. How else could you help yourself feel more powerful, attractive, or sexy?

The more you can cultivate the *feeling* of your desire *before* you have it, the better your chances of making it a reality in your life. If you want to feel more peaceful, for example, you could try a short meditation each day. If you want to feel more successful, you could start by acknowledging the small successes you have every day and begin to move toward taking greater risks that would help you achieve more. If you desire more creative play, spend a little time this week creating a painting, a recipe, a song, or whatever strikes your fancy. It could be coloring in a coloring book or making up a dance in your living room. (I make up dances in my home all the time!)

The Importance of Specificity

A few years ago, I wanted so much to see choreographer Pina Bausch's dance company perform in Brooklyn. But since it was shortly after her death, tickets had sold out fast.

I called the theater to ask if there was any possibility of getting seats. They suggested that my friend and I come down to the theater and see if anybody wanted to give up their tickets. When we got to the theater, we found out that a lot of other people had the same idea. The line was around the block. My heart sunk, but we took our spot in line to take our chances.

Ten minutes before showtime, we were still in line, and it wasn't moving. I thought, *Wouldn't it be nice if somebody walked out of the theater with a ticket they were just giving away?* I allowed myself to believe it was possible, but I didn't tell my friend what I was thinking. He was just along for the ride anyway and didn't care if he got to see the show.

I continued to meditate on the "wouldn't it be nice" scenario, and about five minutes later, lo and behold, somebody walked out of the theater and gave a ticket to someone in line. Except they handed it to someone about five people behind me.

Wait! I said to myself. I realized I had left the most important bit of specificity out of my intention. *I meant wouldn't it be nice if somebody came up and gave a ticket to me!*

So I put myself back into that concentrated, meditative state. *Wouldn't it be nice if somebody walked out of the theater right now and brought a free ticket to this show right to me, to where I'm standing?* I kept repeating this in my head.

And then it happened! My friend saw someone walking toward us with a ticket to give away; he jumped out of the line, grabbed the ticket, and handed it right to me. "Go in," he said. "It's one ticket. The show's starting. Hurry!"

Of course, my efforts don't always work that fast, but it does show the importance of specificity when you're setting an intention or asking for what you want.

Try this as a practice: as you walk through your days, make it a habit to say, "Wouldn't it be nice if . . ." Fill it in with anything you want. It can go from the mundane—"Wouldn't it be nice if the bus arrived right now?"—to the outrageous: "Wouldn't it be nice if Justin Timberlake walked in here and smiled at me?" Let yourself have a moment to envision it, and *be specific!* Have fun with it. Who knows? Justin just might surprise you.

Meanwhile, of course, you'll work on creating your desires in other ways too. Just always remember to avoid "vague land." When we aren't precise about our desires because we're scared they won't work out, we sell ourselves short and limit what's possible. We fear we'll be stuck with something we don't really want and unable to change our minds. Sometimes, we even say,

"I don't really *know* what I want. I'm confused." I have news for you, darling: it's rare that anyone is truly confused about what they want!

You may, however, have different and conflicting feelings. If so, each of your feelings is valid. I'd rather you be honest and say, "I want to be alone, but I also want to be with someone!" Because sometimes, ain't that the truth? You don't have to feel just one way. We're all filled with contradictions.

If you find yourself regularly feeling confused about your desires, try looking at it in a different way. For example, I had a friend who was ready to start a family and have a baby. At the same time, she really wanted to land a Broadway show. If she went after one, it would make the other one nearly impossible. Saying she was conflicted felt more empowering than saying she was "confused" about what she wanted. She simply wanted both.

Nevertheless, specificity is important when we want to create either an inner desire or an outer desire. Knowing what we want to feel is vital, but we also need to be precise in what we envision. Even if your desire is a quality, it helps to think about what your life will *look like* once you've developed that quality. What will your days be like when you have that self-confidence you want or the ability to speak up for yourself?

I worked with someone recently who struggled with specificity. I met her on the Z Living TV show *Altar'd*. I appear on the show as a host and coach for engaged couples who are looking to create an inner and outer transformation before their big day. It's a tremendously rewarding job, where I inevitably fall in love with all the people who allow themselves to be so vulnerable on the show.

While each person sets some pretty big goals, I make sure the individuals are clear on the "why" behind their goals and how they want to feel. The last thing I want is someone focusing their energy on a number on a scale, especially if that number negatively impacts how they feel about themselves. For example, when I asked a woman named Michelle for her "why" goal, she was stuck. So I asked her, "If you released this weight, what would your life look like?"

"I just want to feel more confident, more alive, and have more energy," she said. These were perfectly legitimate inner desires that she expressed, and she knew exactly how she wanted to feel. It was a great first step! It showed that Michelle was aligned with her core values and had enough self-awareness to know that just fitting into a particular pair of jeans wouldn't bring her happiness.

Even so, I could sense that she was reluctant to be more specific about what she really wanted from this experience. She had lost 100 pounds in the past but gained it all back, which was a crushing disappointment for her. She was afraid to set a specific goal now, because what if she didn't reach it? What if it all came back again? Then she'd have to face that same disappointment. Or she might feel embarrassed. It was tough, and I could absolutely understand her reticence.

But I still wanted her to have a compelling and clear vision for her future. The more she practiced holding that vision, the more likely she would be able to achieve and maintain it. Getting more specific about how her desired feelings would "look" in her life was key. So I said, "Let's pretend you're writing a scene for a movie." I worked with her to describe the character in the movie, who was just like Michelle in her ideal life.

"Let's describe this character's ideal day. The alarm goes off. What time is it, and does she hit the snooze button or get up right away?" I asked.

"She gets up right away because she's excited to start her day," Michelle answered.

"Is someone in bed with her, or is she alone?" I asked next.

"Her fiancé is with her."

"How does she feel when she sees him?"

"She's excited that he's next to her."

"What does her bedroom look like?"

Michelle went on to describe her bedroom. Then I asked her to tell me the first action the character would take.

"She puts on a pair of shorts and goes on a long walk."

We kept going with Michelle's ideal day, which allowed her to become more detailed about what she wanted.

Another point that Michelle's story illustrates is the importance of visualization. It helps you create specificity, and it also brings what you want toward you like a magnet. Top athletes have visualized for decades, and studies show that they progress faster as a result than those who don't. Jack Nicklaus, one of the best golfers of all time, visualized his shots in his mind before executing them. Basketball coach Phil Jackson taught visualization exercises to players like Michael Jordan and Kobe Bryant, which helped their teams win 11 championships over the years.

When I was in my college dance program, we'd learn new choreography every day. So at night before bed, I'd visualize myself doing the steps over and over. It didn't just help me remember the choreography; it helped me perform the way I visualized it.

You may have visualized before, but remember that it's a skill. You can never get too good at it, and the more you do it, the better you'll become.

Meditation #1: Hone Your Visualization Skills

Let's try some visualizing. If you find it difficult to "see" what you're imagining in your mind's eye, don't worry. Some of us are more kinesthetic than visual, which means we tend to feel more than we see. Just allow yourself to feel what you're imagining, and use all your senses if you can. If you're on a beach, for example, feel the sand under the feet, the heat of the sun, the smell of the salt in the air, and the taste of the tropical fruit cocktail you're sipping.

Also, make sure you aren't just observing yourself. It's easy to feel separate from the experience, as though you're watching yourself go through the motions. Instead, try to experience it as though you're seeing it happen through your own eyes, looking out at the world around you.

To do this meditation, you can record yourself reading it and play it back, or you can visit my website for an audio version at www.erinstutland.com/gifts. Just keep your eyes closed throughout the meditation so that you don't interrupt your relaxation. You'll only need about 10 minutes.

1. Close your eyes, and begin to relax each part of your body, starting with your feet and legs and moving up to your torso, chest, arms, shoulders, neck, head, and face. You don't even have to know how to relax your body. Just tell yourself each part is relaxing.
2. Choose any desire you have. It can be anything from more self-confidence to a new job to a relationship to a vacation. (If you still aren't sure what you want, choose one of the answers from your dig-for-gold exploration in Journaling Exercise #2, question numbers 2 and 3.)
3. Imagine that this desire has already manifested. It's done and complete! You're now the you of the future who is enjoying your success. What does the life of this future look like? Are you in a home, an apartment, a park, or standing on a stage? Imagine the place where you'll be standing when you have what you want. Either see it in your mind's eye, or feel it. Envision the details of this place. What's in front of you? What are the colors? Are there people around you?
4. Take a look to your right. What's there? Is there a window, door, wallpaper, or trees? Then slowly turn your head and look to the left. What do you see?
5. Look down at your feet. See them standing in this place that shows you've manifested what you want. What kind of shoes are you wearing, if any at all? Feel yourself standing there strong and solid.

6. Turn inward. How do you feel now that you've accomplished this? Do you feel proud, excited, or confident? Allow the feeling to bubble up. You might even feel a bit of anxiety. That's natural. The truth is that if you aren't a little afraid, you aren't dreaming big enough. So let those butterflies be an indication that you're on the right path. (If you aren't feeling butterflies, don't worry. Just make your goal bigger next time.)
7. Is there anyone else there with you in the future? Who's the first person who comes to mind—someone who would share this achievement with you? See or feel this person in front of you, and take a moment to look into their eyes. Are they looking back at you with love and pride? What stands out to you about this person right now? What is their most prominent physical feature? Make their face as clear and real to you as you can. Then notice their energy. Is it excited or calm? Listen and hear anything this person wants to say to you in this moment. Take in their words.
8. How is this future life tangibly different from your current life? Does it feel very different? Allow yourself to spend some time hanging out in this feeling. It can be tempting to want to cut it short. We often struggle to sit solidly in positive feelings, so please drink in the feeling of success and happiness. You've done it! You've created what you wanted.
9. Hold on to the feeling as long as you can. When you're ready, slowly open your eyes.

Let It Go

The most difficult step in creating what you want is declaring your desire and then letting it go. As we've discussed, it's important to get specific and think about what your desire will look like. But if you hold too tightly to that image, you might miss the fulfillment of your wish if it arrives looking a bit different than you imagined. That mistake almost cost me my wonderful marriage!

When I was working to manifest a relationship, I made a list of what I wanted the man in my life to be like, including how he would treat me and how I'd feel. But the idea that I would marry a man who had been an elementary school classmate was, at first, too strange. It wasn't the way I had envisioned it, but there was wisdom beyond what my little mind could conceive.

The paradox of manifesting is to get specific and then to let the specificity go. But when you let it go, you allow for the form to be even better.

When I was in my 20s, I wanted to land a role in a TV show, film, or play. But when I checked in with my feelings and my core values, I realized that what I really wanted was to have full creative expression, to share that creativity, and to have an impact on others through the expression of my creativity.

When I started my own business, I didn't think it would provide this expression for me, but it did. I'd always wanted to be a working artist. I just never dreamed my medium of expression would be a business of my own since it didn't look exactly the way we tend to think of art. But there it is, and I love it!

So allow the form of your desire to be different or even more than you envisioned. After all, stretching beyond what we've experienced thus far can be difficult because we have no frame of reference. If we don't let riches come our way, we'll never expand past where we are now. That's one of the main reasons why knowing the *feeling* you'll get from your desire is so important.

So set your desire, get specific, imagine how you'll feel, see the form you'd like it to take, and allow it to come in a different form that's even better! Got it?

We'll work a bit more on letting it go in Chapter 8, but right now let's solidify your intention with our first mantra and movement sequence. Remember our mantra?

I let my desire guide me
I do what feels right
I stay true to my vision
I keep love in sight!

Movement with Mantras

Now it's time to bring your body's energy to your desires as you work out and chant your mantra. When you say the words, think about a feeling you want to cultivate. For example, if you want to feel more courage, think about that as you say the mantra. (You can also, of course, choose to think about an item or experience you want, like a new job, but I suggest working with the feeling you believe it will bring.)

If you still aren't quite clear about what you want to create, simply make your vision about feeling good. Part of this sequence is about trusting your vision and your own gut—your intuition. So ideas may come to the surface as you move with the mantra. If they do, trust them!

As you move and say the mantra, fill your body with the feeling you're trying to create. As best you can, feel it coursing and pulsating throughout your body. Let your passion and enthusiasm for what you want rise and build inside you. Even if you're trying to create greater peace, you can be enthusiastic about it. Let this feeling feed your movement so that you're even more physically and emotionally energized.

You might want to remind yourself how the movements and mantras work together by referring back to the Q&A section in Chapter 1. I have also provided a video of this pattern so we can do it together. You can access it at www.erinstutland.com/gifts.

MANTRA IN MOTION #1

You'll be amazed at what five minutes can do for you in terms of shifting your perception and your mood. It's a great starting point! Of course, if you're ready for more, you can increase the length of the sequence by cycling through the movements and mantras two times for a 10-minute workout or three times for a 15-minute workout.

It's important that while you are moving your body, you allow your breath to soothe your mind and your body. I call it "staying easy." If an exercise feels difficult for you, notice where your mind wants to go. Does it rush to blame, worry, fear, or doubt? Pay attention, and gently bring your thoughts back to the mantras.

Also remember not to worry if you say the lines of the mantras at the exact right moment or with the exact right movements. It doesn't matter! Your energy and joy are what truly count!

Are you ready to get started? Let's begin with our mantra on desire:

I let my desire guide me
I do what feels right
I stay true to my vision
I keep love in sight!

Move 1: Plié Reach

Line 1: *I let my desire guide me*

"I let my desire guide me"

1. "I let my desire guide me." Stand with your feet a little wider than hips' distance apart. Turn your toes out slightly. As you do, let the words "I let my desire guide me" really sink in to your mind and heart. Allow the desire you uncovered in this chapter to be in the forefront of your mind. What does it feel like to allow *desire* to be your guiding force?
2. Bend your knees into a squat, and bring your hands up to your heart with your palms touching as in a prayer. You may want to break the mantra into two parts. On the way down into your squat, say, "I let . . ."
3. Rise up, bringing your hands into a "V" position. On your way up, you can say, ". . . my desire guide me." Feel an opening in your heart as you say the words and complete the movements. *This is one rep.*
4. Repeat this movement and mantra 16 times.

Move 2: Chair Pose Rising

Line 2: *I do what feels right*

"I do what feels right"

1. "I do what feels right." How often do you ignore your inner voice? Are you willing to take action on what feels right for you? Let this mantra sink in. Starting with your feet together, bend your knees as if sitting in a chair, and swing your arms behind you. Sit down as low as you can. Say, "I do what feels . . ."
2. Straighten your legs, and swing your arms up over your head. Be sure to relax your shoulders. On the way up, say, ". . . right." *This is one rep.*
3. Find a gentle flow between these two positions.
4. Repeat this movement and mantra 16 times.

Move 1: Plié Reach

Line 3: *I stay true to my vision*

"I stay true to my vision"

1. "I stay true to my vision." Do you feel you do stay true to your vision? If not, this mantra will help you change that! Are you willing to now stay true to the desire you focused on earlier in the chapter? As you think about your desire, stand with your feet a little wider than hips' distance apart. Turn your toes out slightly.
2. Bend your knees into a squat, and bring your hands up to your heart with your palms touching as in a prayer. Say, "I stay true to my . . ."
3. Rise up, bringing your hands into a "V" position. Feel your heart opening as you do so, and say, ". . . vision." *This is one rep.*
4. Find a nice flow between these two movements as you say the third line of the mantra.
5. Repeat this movement 16 times.

Move 2: Chair Pose Rising

Line 4: *I keep love in sight*

"I keep love in sight"

1. "I keep love in sight." What if you approached your newfound desire with love rather than trying to push or force it? You could let it blossom and bloom on its own. Starting with your feet together, bend your knees as you would if sitting in a chair, and swing your arms behind you.
2. Sit down as low as you can. Say, "I keep love in . . ." Straighten your legs, and swing your arms up over your head. Be sure to relax your shoulders. On the way up, say, ". . . sight." *This is one rep.*
3. Move through the chair pose to standing in a steady flow while saying, "I keep love in sight."
4. Repeat this movement and mantra 16 times.

Now you're going to put all the movements together for 10 cycles. Simply alternate between Move 1 and Move 2, taking care to pay attention to the transition between the two movements to help it stay smooth. You should now be comfortable with the moves and have the full four-line mantra memorized. Do one move with one line at a time. It will flow like this:

Move 1: Plié Reach
Mantra : *I let my desire guide me*
(Pause, take a breath, and bring your right foot in to prepare for the next move.)

Move 2: Chair Pose Rising
Mantra: *I do what feels right*
(Pause, take a breath, and step your right foot out to prepare for the next move.)

Move 1: Plié Reach
Mantra: *I stay true to my vision*
(Pause, take a breath, and bring your left foot out to prepare for the next move.)

Move 2: Chair Pose Rising
Mantra: *I keep love in sight*
(Pause, take a breath, and step your left foot to prepare to start the cycle again.)

That is *one* cycle. You will repeat this whole cycle 10 times. Take your time to transition between the two movements until it becomes more seamless for you.

While this may seem like a lot at first, I want you to dig in and stay committed. If it feels challenging, allow the mantras to support you through the challenge. That's *exactly* why you're doing this. You're conditioning your mind to associate a challenge with empowered thoughts!

RELEASE RESISTANCE

"I can't seem to get started." "I have a lot of enthusiasm in the beginning, but then I lose motivation and stop." "I procrastinate so much that some of my most exciting projects get put off for years." I hear statements like these from my clients all the time when they try something new or want to move forward in their lives. The culprit is resistance—that old friend that we all know so well.

Resistance can show up in disguise too. It won't be wearing a trench coat and a hat covering its eyes, but it might arrive as anger, frustration, anxiety, sadness, or fatigue. Sometimes, resistance brings up certain behaviors in us like procrastination, complaining, gossiping, compulsive eating, or rebelliousness. I learned that complaining is one of my go-to resistance tactics when I caught myself grumbling and moaning to a friend instead of taking positive action.

According to Steven Pressfield, author of *The War of Art: Break Through the Blocks and Win Your Inner Creative Battles*, resistance is actually a good sign because it shows up when we have a dream. And resistance often rears its head with a vengeance exactly when we're getting super close to achieving that dream.

Wow, did I see resistance in action when I first started my business. I ran a four-week in-person program, and everyone felt all fired up the first week. They set their intentions for the month and were ready to take on the world!

Then week two came along, and I saw a small drop in attendance. That week, we talked about our beliefs and what held us back from our set goals. (Incidentally, we're going to do that in the next chapter.)

Then the third week rolled around, and inevitably, we had a significant drop-off rate.

Of course, the fourth week, some people showed up again, trying to make up for what they'd missed. But by that time, they'd lost the momentum they'd built in those first couple of weeks toward making the changes they wanted in their lives. So why did so many of them drop out during the third week? I refer to this as the three-quarter slump!

We begin going after something with a lot of enthusiasm. After all, starting anything new is exciting. This excitement carries us along while we're working toward our dream, but just as we get close to fulfilling it (usually about three-quarters of the way there), resistance comes to the surface and derails us. That's because resistance is actually a specific kind of fear. We'll talk about fear a lot throughout the book, but resistance merits its own chapter because it's a powerful obstacle that can keep us from achieving our dreams.

Now, bear in mind that resistance is well intentioned. It thinks it's keeping us safe. The problem is that it also keeps us "safely" on this side of what we want.

Resistance offers a desirable "payoff." I don't necessarily mean a positive one. As strange as it sounds, negative payoffs are sometimes more desirable. For example, the surface payoff for choosing *not* to go to the gym is that we get to sit on the couch. That's certainly more comfortable than a hard workout. Another payoff of not going to the gym is not having to deal with life if our body changes. Maybe we're afraid that as a result of the change, we'll attract more attention, and the prospects of that are scary.

The payoff for not taking action on our dreams is often rooted in the fear of the unknown because the scared child in each of us longs for stability and safety. But stability and safety aren't as desirable to the wiser part of us that wants to grow and experience life fully. In order to grow, we have to risk failure. Fear of that risk is at the heart of resistance.

Sometimes, resistance shows up as our inner critic. We relate to it as if it's individual and personal, but as Steven Pressfield says, it's actually universal and impersonal.[1] The voice of resistance may hone in on what we fear is true: "You'll never be able to do that!" "You aren't any good at this." "Why do you bother trying when you know it won't work out?" But the truth is that everybody has this same voice! Me, you, your neighbor, your favorite teacher, and even people who are considered the best in their fields, from Albert Einstein to Meryl Streep. To my knowledge, no one has been exempted from this critical voice. It's loud enough at the start of a new endeavor, but it gets louder when we get to that three-quarter point. And it *really* goes for broke when we get close to making our dream a reality.

Stop right now and think about a goal you haven't reached. How does your personal brand of resistance show up? Do you feel tired? Do you tell yourself you aren't good enough? Do you feel defeated before you even start? Do you tell yourself that you keep finding roadblocks "out there"? Do you procrastinate?

Each of us has our own personal brand of resistance and a payoff it gives us. Your first journaling exercise in this chapter will help you pinpoint what those are for you. Once you know, you can begin to move past these roadblocks. Thankfully, it doesn't take a Jedi mind trick. You don't have to "Om Shanti" your way past resistance. You don't need to "fix" yourself.

You simply need to *stop and notice* that what you *are* doing is a form of *not doing* what you know you need and want to do! You've said no to an activity that will help you reach your goal, and you've said yes to an activity that won't get you there, even if that "activity" is nothing at all.

Your resistance might feel like a brick wall, but remember that it isn't a real brick wall. It's an imaginary one that you've created inside your own head and heart, and the good news is

1 Steven Pressfield, "Resistance and Self-Loathing," StevenPressfield.com, Nov. 2013, accessed May 24, 2018, https://stevenpressfield.com/2013/11/resistance-and-self-loathing/.

that you don't need a jackhammer to take it down. You simply need to get familiar with your own brand of resistance. When you catch it as it begins to rear its head, remind yourself that it isn't personal. It's simply like a familiar song that plays every time you get close to your dream.

If you stop taking your resistance so personally, you'll be less likely to be thrown off by it. You'll just recognize the familiar tune and think, *Oh, this is the music that comes on every time I get close to what I want.* Through this recognition, you'll be able to keep working toward your goal.

Then you can move into a state of flow. Psychologist Mihaly Csikszentmihalyi describes flow as "complete immersion" in what you're doing. You're "tuned in" to what you want, and you keep putting one foot in front of the other with your eyes on the prize.

When I'm in flow, I'm so involved in what I'm doing that I can't believe how much time has passed. I feel light in my body and free in my mind. I feel inspired and full of energy. I stop reaching outside of myself for solutions because I trust that I already have everything I need. Ideas then come to me without effort.

Moving into a state of flow is possible for everyone, but it takes some practice to stop taking the voice of resistance so personally. The more you become familiar with your own brand of resistance, and the more you practice moving forward despite it, the easier it becomes to move into flow.

But remember what I said in the previous chapter: if you aren't a little afraid, you aren't dreaming big enough. For this reason, fear and resistance will likely never go away completely. The exercises in this chapter will help you resist *less* so that you won't be as likely to hit that three-quarter slump. Then, in spite of whatever resistance may remain, you'll move through it toward your dream. So let's make a pact to practice moving into flow as often as we possibly can, and let's start with our mantra for this chapter.

First, the mantra leads you to tune in. When you tune out the inner critic and tune in to yourself and your desires, you're more present in the moment—more in flow. I even like to think of it as tuning in to the magic of life and all that it has to offer.

From there, you step further into that wonderful feeling of flow, accepting that you have everything you could possibly need at this moment to step forward. At the end, you finally let go of *at least most of* your resistance.

I am tuned in
I step into the flow
I have all that I need
The rest I let go!

Repeat it with me one more time:

I am tuned in
I step into the flow
I have all that I need
The rest I let go!

Three Common Causes of Resistance

Most of the time, we express our brand of resistance unconsciously. It's almost like going into a trance. We sit down in front of the TV with a box of cookies—hardly even aware that we're doing it—instead of meditating or finishing the creation of our website.

That's why self-awareness is key if we want to leave resistance behind. If we learn to identify what's happening when we resist what we want, it's much easier to get the flow going. So let's break down some of the most common causes of resistance to help you recognize your own personal brand of resistance and the payoff you get from it.

Being Overwhelmed. It's easy to get overwhelmed by all we have to do to achieve our goal. There are so many steps to get there that we can't imagine ourselves ever finishing them all. It's what I felt when I started writing this book! I'm supposed to write more than 50,000 words? Did you say *50,000*? Whoa, that's a lot! It's enough to make me want to go back to bed and pull the sheets over my head.

But when I'm thinking about all 50,000 of those words, I'm far away from the moment. My mind has raced ahead to a place where I'm looking back at the long stretch between the beginning and the end. I can't even see the beginning from that vantage point. Who wouldn't feel overwhelmed by that?

If, on the other hand, I stay in the moment rather than worry about the future, I can write one sentence at a time. Then, before I know it, the whole book is done. When I'm at the end, that long stretch will look a lot shorter.

Sometimes, the overwhelmed version of resistance says, "It will take too long." Again, this only happens when we're not in the moment. If I told myself writing a book would take too long, I'd surely never get started. I know someone who felt three years of graduate school would take too long, but eight years later, she still longed for that degree. If she'd gone when the impulse struck her, she could have already enjoyed the fruits of her education for five whole years! If we just get started, we'll reach the finish line much faster than if we resist and procrastinate.

When we're not in the moment, we're much more susceptible to resistance. When we're present in the moment, we're much more open to ease, inspiration, creativity, ideas, and love—good old flow.

Trauma and Exhaustion. When we go through trauma, it's natural for resistance to come up. We're emotionally exhausted and in a recovery phase, so it's hard to muster up the energy and courage to go for what we want. My client Sara became resistant to taking good care of herself physically and mentally because she was emotionally spent. And for good reason. She'd lost her job, gone back to school, had a health scare, and experienced both a betrayal and a death in a relatively short period of time. That's a lot to handle. As a result, she stopped preparing healthy meals for herself, had no energy for moving her body, and stopped spending time with friends who could lift her spirits.

"After all that 'rough life stuff,' I'm having such a hard time moving forward and rebuilding the energy I used to have for life and creativity and taking care of myself," Sara told me.

When my sister-in-law-to-be suddenly passed away just six weeks before our wedding, I experienced something similar. It was grief and transition at the same time. Everyone in the family was happy about our wedding while also feeling intense pain about the loss of someone we all loved so much. Understandably, in the aftermath, I found myself sapped of energy.

Sitting down to do my morning pages had always provided me with a boost of energy to get my day going, but suddenly, I could barely bring myself to sit and write. I was too tired to work out, and I had little creative output in my business. But I did my best to keep showing up with whatever I had to give. Instead of writing for 30 minutes, I tried to write for 10. Instead of creating a new product for my business, I resold a product already in my arsenal. Instead of writing long blog posts, I put together bite-size posts. I didn't have a lot of wind, but I kept going, even if I completed just one small task in a day. And every now and then, the act of moving that little bit brought me a gust of wind that signaled the return of my normal strong breezes.

Sure, you may need a period of inactivity during your recovery, but there will come a time when you have to push forward again so that you don't move into a permanent state of inaction. While there is no set time frame for how long that period of quietness will last, you may start to feel glimmers of sunshine through the darkness. Perhaps you find yourself laughing or smiling a bit more. It's important to be gentle with yourself, but you can experiment with pushing yourself just a little bit to begin to change your course. If it feels like too much, sink back into your inactivity as needed. Then, in a short while, try pushing yourself again until the movement feels doable. (Of course, if you do begin to feel stuck in the emotional pain, please get yourself some professional help if at all possible.)

Most importantly, if the wind has been knocked out of your sails, do what you can to show up to the sea anyway. Put your boat in the water even if you just sit there in the beginning. By keeping yourself available, even if the wind is absent at first, you'll make tiny waves in your subconscious. Before you know it, being out at sea will become enjoyable again, and your wind will come back to move you toward your goals.

Perfectionism. This is a big one for me. I worry that I won't reach my goal "perfectly." I'm afraid I won't know how to do what's required for my dream. So I stop dead in my tracks. I've resisted sending out blog posts and telling my online audience about new products, for example, because of the fear they weren't perfect enough. *Maybe people will think my ideas are weird or crazy,* I thought. *If I only keep tinkering, I can make them at least closer to perfect.* But, of course, no creation is ever perfect. I'll bet even Picasso was dissatisfied with some of the works we consider to be his greatest. It's almost inevitable that we see ways to improve our work only after it's completed. That's why at some point, we have to have the courage to stop resisting and let our work be finished, knowing that perfection is an ideal we'll never reach.

When I finally stopped requiring that my work be perfect, what I produced got better each time, and I felt prouder of every blog post and product. A study conducted in an art class had similar results. The class was divided into two groups. Group A was going to be graded on a single masterpiece for the year. Group B was assigned to make as many pieces of art as possible. The more they made, the better their grade would be because it was based on quantity. Guess what happened? Group B not only made more art, but they had a deeper level of satisfaction with their work because it got better and better with each piece.

So let's redefine "perfect" right now. It derives from the Latin word *perfectus,* which actually means "finished or complete." I now suggest to my students that if they've finished or completed a task—in whatever form—it's perfect.

This is how we turn perfectionism on its head. Rather than imposing some difficult standard on what we do, we call the completion of each task "perfect." So practice doing things "perfectly" by simply calling them so because they're finished—and that might mean finishing just one small step on your list toward a larger goal.

When you write an email, declare it perfect. When you brush your teeth, pronounce them as perfectly clean. Even if you have a frustrating conversation with a customer service representative or a fight with your partner, declare it perfect. The experience has taught you something, even if you don't know what you learned yet.

In the next exercise, you'll explore your personal brand of resistance. As you write your answers to the journaling questions, think about our mantra for this chapter. Can you see how it can help you move past resistance into flow?

I am tuned in
I step into the flow
I have all that I need
The rest I let go!

Journaling Exercise #3: Your Personal Brand of Resistance

1. Answer the following questions to explore how both resistance and flow show up in your life.

   Where are you in flow?

   1. What are you enthusiastic about doing?
   2. What tasks do you find easy to finish?
   3. What do you always find time for?
   4. What are you doing when you find it easy to meet a deadline?
   5. When you arrive on time, what are you getting ready to do?
   6. What are you doing when you don't procrastinate?

Where are you in resistance?

1. What do you spend more time doing than you'd like?
2. What do you tend to say yes to when you'd rather say no?
3. What do you wish you had more time to do?
4. When you're late, what are you getting ready to do?
5. When you procrastinate, what are you getting ready to do?
6. What tasks do you struggle to finish?

2. Review your answers for patterns. Is your personal brand of resistance primarily about feeling overwhelmed, trauma, perfectionism, or something else? Write down what you discover.
3. Now ask yourself what payoff you can discern from your answers. What do you get from your personal brand of resistance? Do you get to stay small and avoid the risk of failure? Write down what you discover.

We'll use the movements with mantras to charge through these blocks, but now that you know your own resistance patterns, you won't be able to fool yourself as easily that procrastinating or binging on Netflix make sense. In the meantime, if you catch yourself resisting, take a deep breath and try to forgive yourself.

From Resistance into Flow

There are times in your life when resistance either doesn't show up at all or you move through it with ease and reach your goal—when your state of flow is effortless. You have a right to feel proud when that happens. Wouldn't you like to have a soccer announcer around to shout "Gooooooooaaaaaaaaaallllllllll" in those moments?

But what about when flow seems to be nowhere in sight? My client Holly has a particular resistance pattern of getting organized and then becoming paralyzed. "I keep saying I'll start on Monday. I'll start when I get new sneakers. I'll start when the holidays are over," she says. She labels herself as "lazy," but it's really fear that has her stuck in resistance and blocking her flow. Her negative payoff from the pattern is never having to deal with failure if she doesn't reach her goal. But she's definitely never going to succeed if she doesn't let herself get started.

So I asked her, "Are there any tasks in life that you find easy to start?"

"Yes," she said. "Usually, when someone is in need or I'm doing something for someone else, I jump right in. If it involves my kids or my parents or work, I'm up to my elbows. I struggle with taking time to work on myself."

So when someone is counting on Holly, she sees it through. If there isn't any pressure because she's the only person who would be affected, she resists. I have a similar problem, so I make sure I always have a deadline. Even if no one else has told me when I have to be finished, I give myself a specific date. I like to say, "If it hasn't been written down and scheduled, it will never get done." For Holly, I suggested she find an accountability partner to help her move from resistance into flow—someone she'd report to about her progress—and it helped her see goals to fruition.

Sometimes, like Holly, we can "borrow" skills we use when we're not resistant and apply them to the times we do resist. I used to be late frequently when I'd get together with friends. It was embarrassing and made me feel like a slacker. Yet I was *never* late for auditions. I always got there at least 15 minutes early, so I knew I was capable of being on time. Why wasn't I doing that with my friends? First, I had to ask myself: "Are you willing to change and be on time for non-work-related meetings?" My answer was yes.

I watched myself when getting ready to meet friends versus getting ready for auditions. When I was preparing for a casual meeting, I kept trying to finish little tasks rather than start getting ready when I knew I should. I didn't do that before auditions because I knew how important it was to be on time. So I had to make a commitment to get ready at the exact right time before a casual social meeting. I had to be disciplined enough to stop myself from doing unnecessary tasks. It took a few tries, but I was able to make that change. Now I leave my house on time no matter what.

Take a look at the answers you wrote in the last journaling exercise. Can you find a way to apply what's working to what isn't working? Let's say you love listening to music, and it helps you achieve a state of flow. Maybe you could start an activity you've been putting off with some music. That might be enough to give you the jump start you need.

Bear in mind that even if you move into flow, it doesn't mean you won't experience an obstacle or glitch on occasion. Still, from a place of flow, you'll be less likely to freeze when an obstacle crosses your path. It becomes a problem-solving opportunity rather than an anxiety generator or an excuse to stop. You'll stay relaxed and keep moving forward, even if you have to move a little bit more slowly. Remember the lines of our mantra: "I have all that I need. The rest I let go."

Of course, if you find yourself moving in and out of resistance and flow, don't worry. You're just flexing your muscles and learning the ropes. The more you consciously work to counteract your resistance, the easier you'll find it to *flow* into flow.

To some degree, moving into flow requires stepping into the void. I know that sounds scary, but again, it's only because it's an unknown. A few years ago, I wrote and performed a one-woman show. When I sat down to write it, I was faced with a scary blank page. At first, it was hard to get started. I resisted. I wrote in my schedule, "Work on writing the show for one hour on Sunday at 3:00 P.M." But when Sunday rolled around, I distracted myself with other activities.

I had hired a director to work with me, and when I told him my dilemma, he said, "Instead of telling yourself to write for one hour, how about telling yourself to 'step into the void' for one hour?" At first, I didn't understand what he meant, but after a little coaxing, it became clear that I simply needed to give myself permission to sit in front of my computer screen without knowing what would happen. I could free myself from needing all the answers to just start typing and be curious about whatever came out. Maybe I'd write something I could use. Maybe not. The magical thing is that voids long to be filled. So even though you don't know what will happen once you step in, "something" usually comes forth from taking that action.

When I put this simple action of "step into the void on Sunday at 3:00 P.M." on my schedule, it completely changed how I approached that time. It was no longer this looming pressure that I had to write something brilliant in that hour. I could simply show up, and if nothing came out but gobbledygook, that was okay. Of course, as a result, I started doing some of my best work. Why? Because I'd moved past resistance and perfectionism into flow.

As Neale Donald Walsch once said, "Life begins at the end of your comfort zone." So trust that there's something greater waiting for you, but you have to step into the void beyond your comfort zone to find that something greater. You risk finding nothing at all, but think about this: nothing simply leaves you no worse off than you are right now.

Let's take a deep breath and try stepping into that void. Don't worry; I'll be with you the whole way.

Meditation #2: Visit the Void

In this meditation, we're going to release your resistance and make the void a less scary place to be. Again, you can visit www .erinstutland.com/gifts for an audio of the meditation, or you can record yourself reading it. If you don't tend to visualize, simply *feel* what I describe to the best of your ability.

1. Close your eyes and slowly relax each part of your body from your feet all the way up to the top of your head. Simply say, "I relax my feet, I relax my legs," and so forth.
2. When you've finished relaxing your body from toe to head as best you can, imagine yourself in a peaceful place. Maybe you're on the beach or in a garden—whatever you prefer is perfect. Allow that peaceful feeling to float through your body and mind as you breathe in and out. Feel your breathing become easier and calmer.
3. Imagine that there's an ornate, golden door. Maybe it's a door where a door shouldn't be, but here it is anyway. Behind that door is the void. It's where you want to go because through that void is the fulfillment of a goal you want to reach. But on this side of the door, your resistance is stopping you.
4. Imagine that your resistance has taken the form of a coat, and it's now wrapped tightly around you. Weaved into the coat are the thoughts, fears, and ideas that are holding you back. They're close to you, but they are *not you*. As a result, the coat begins to feel heavy and too hot. It becomes harder and harder to move freely until you can't wear that coat for another second. So go ahead and take that thing off! As you do, you're shedding your resistance. Let it fall to the ground. You don't need it anymore. There now . . . isn't that better? Don't you feel more comfortable? Don't you feel free? Nothing's holding you back now.
5. Think of a specific goal you want to reach. If none comes to mind, that's okay. You can just allow one to come to you in the moment after you enter the void.
6. Allow yourself to go ahead and open the door. Take a deep breath, and step inside. It's okay. I'm here with you. In this void is a room that's filled with the fruition of your goal. What you see in this

room will show you what you have to gain when you stop resisting.

7. The room is dark, so you might feel afraid. But you can do it. Step further inside. Feel around on the wall. There's a light switch. Flip it on, and look around. This is your future after you've let go of the resistance and received what you want. Feel the freedom, the flow, and the happiness of having achieved what you set out to do. Spend as much time here as you like, and allow yourself to drink in the details.
8. When you're ready, open your eyes, and bask in that feeling of achievement. You may want to take some notes so you don't forget what you experienced in the void.

The next time you find yourself in resistance, remember this feeling. You might even decide to go back to this meditation and step into the void again. It can help to dissipate your fears and move you into flow.

This is a good time to recall our mantra:

I am tuned in
I step into the flow
I have all that I need
The rest I let go!

Take a "Soul Stroll"

Years ago, when I ended a long-term relationship, I found myself brooding on what I *could* have done differently and what he *should* have done differently. Before long, I realized that I couldn't change the past, so this kind of thinking was pointless. So each day, I dedicated 20 minutes to a walk outside to connect to the intention of healing my mind and heart. I started to call these walks my "Soul Strolls." Soon after, I created special playlists that included upbeat music along with mantras to address the issues that the breakup brought up for me, like feeling that the relationship didn't work because I wasn't perfect enough. I soon found that I felt better and stopped replaying the past in my head. My Soul Strolls helped me moved on.

Studies show that even a nine-minute walk helps to improve concentration, focus, and attention span. I've found that a Soul Stroll is one of the most effective ways to move out of resistance and into flow. It can help you reconnect to yourself so that you feel more centered, grounded, and at ease in your body. And it releases feel-good endorphins! Even during the winter months, there's nothing better, more refreshing, or good for the spirit than getting some fresh air during a stroll.

So bundle up if necessary, and head out of the house for ten minutes away and ten minutes back. I'm willing to bet you'll feel recharged and refreshed after. For an extra boost, download my free Soul Stroll playlist: www.erinstutland.com/free-soul-stroll.

Your Unique Relationship with Time

How often do you say, "I don't have enough time," "There wasn't enough time to do it," or "When am I going to find the time to do that?" Let's make another pact to remove phrases like that from our vocabulary.

The truth is that we *make* time for what we want to do. We don't "find" it or "manage" it. There's a finite amount of time available to us every day, but we have just as much time as Ruth Bader Ginsburg, Barack Obama, Oprah, or Lin-Manuel Miranda. They've just learned to use their time more wisely than the rest of us.

When we want to accomplish anything, we simply need to make it a priority. We have to say yes to working toward our goal rather than distracting ourselves with YouTube videos.

I know you have real obligations that take up a lot of your time, but if you want to say yes to a particular goal, you'll find a way. Even people with a house full of kids and no money for a sitter find a way to write books and finish important projects. They might have to work slowly, but they do it. Yes, it means moving out of resistance, but if they can do it, so can you!

The key obstacle here is our relationship with time. Each of us has our own unique way of spending time—and wasting it. But most of us don't recognize our preferences, and we don't accept them as our reality. Instead, we impose an ideal on ourselves, creating unrealistic schedules that set us up for failure. For example, it might sound inspiring to schedule a meditation or exercise session at 6:00 A.M., but I know myself well enough to know that's never going to happen. I can't peel myself out of bed before 7:00 A.M. at the earliest unless I absolutely have to.

We simply have to know our limitations and set our own priorities based on what works for us. My clients are often resistant to setting aside "me time"—moments for self-care that prevent burnout. But with so many obligations for others, how often do we put our own health and sanity at the bottom of the priority list?

My client Tina is a disabled single parent with two young adults at home, and when she signed up for one of my courses, she was also going to postsecondary school full-time! Tina was getting sick and falling behind in her classes. Yet she still learned how to better manage her time and prioritize self-care. She decided to make "not having a goal" her goal, and she stepped into the void.

For Tina, stepping into the void meant letting go of perfectionism, which also gave her more time for herself. "Instead of worrying about cleaning my kitchen," she says, "I'm now okay(ish) with letting dishes sit while I Soul Stroll with my pup in the mornings. I'm in the pool two to three mornings a week, I make a meal plan by the month so that everyone knows ahead of time what to expect, and I have a delivery service bringing my groceries so that I don't have to 'waste time' shopping." The negative "I have no time" mantra is no longer a part of Tina's resistance vocabulary.

Then there's my client Peter, who says, "I had a massive aversion to time management. I didn't even own a calendar or diary. What sort of boring corporate person is bound by a calendar when unstructured days are awesome and you can improvise?" But Peter's lack of structure was interfering with his ability to reach his goals.

Still, he had to concede that he was a creative type, and he couldn't just become a 100 percent structured person. He had to strike a balance between structure and improvisation so that his free-flowing nature was still allowed to breathe.

So be careful not to force yourself into a structure that doesn't work for you. That will just bring up even more resistance! Instead, work on finding an organic way to bring more structure into your life. With that in mind, let's evaluate your personal preferences related to time so that you can use it wisely and move more easily into flow.

Journaling Exercise #4: Your Time Preferences

Write down your answers to these questions:

1. Are you a morning or night person?
2. What's the most productive time of day for you? If you aren't sure, start paying attention! You can do this by making a note of how you feel every hour on the hour (except while you sleep, of course). Do this for two or three days to uncover your patterns.
3. Do you like to stay busy and work fast, or do you like a slow pace?
4. Do you prefer to concentrate for long or short periods of time?
5. Do you like to have plenty of time to achieve a goal, or do you work better under pressure?
6. Do you make gut decisions, or do you like to weigh all your options?
7. Do you concentrate better with quiet or background noise?

The next time you set a deadline or make a list toward reaching a goal, take a look at your answers to these questions and take them into account. Don't fill your to-do list if you prefer a slow pace. Give yourself frequent breaks if you find it hard to concentrate for long periods. Schedule the tasks that cause you the most resistance during your high-productivity times. Then you won't be fighting against your ability to be in flow.

Let's say you're a night person who prefers to concentrate for short periods of time. You like to work fast but not under pressure, and you tend to make gut decisions. You also prefer quiet while you work. You might schedule some of your tasks in the evening when you have the most energy. You'll break down the tasks into small increments so that you don't have to concentrate for long periods. You might even find that you have to finish just a few tasks each night until you complete all of them on your list. Maybe Monday night, you'll brainstorm ideas. Tuesday night, you'll go through them and decide on one to implement. Wednesday night, you'll make a list of tasks related to that one idea.

If you're someone who likes to work for longer periods of time, you might do all of those tasks in one sitting. Experiment until you find what works best for you! The key is to not force yourself to be who you aren't.

MANTRA IN MOTION #2

I can imagine that some of you are thinking, "All of these tips are great, Erin, but how do I *actually make myself move forward when I'm stuck in resistance*?" Yeah, I know. There comes a moment when you just have to *do it*. So here's my remedy: when all is said and done, the best way I know how to shift from resistance to flow is to *move your body*. After all, your body can only move in the present moment. You can't stay stuck in worries about the past or the future, especially when you're saying mantras while you move. In that case, your body, heart, and mind are much too busy in the now.

So let's get your body moving with your mantra, and say goodbye to your resistance.

Your Resistance Mantra

I am tuned in
I step into the flow
I have all that I need
The rest I let go!

Move 1: Prayer Fold

Line 1: *I am tuned in*
This first mantra is about tuning in to the calm, steady voice within you while tuning out any extra noise or thoughts that don't serve you. Once you feel comfortable with this movement, it helps to close your eyes to block out any external stimulation.

"I am tuned in"

1. Start by standing with your feet together and your hands by your side. Feel your heart lifting as your shoulders melt down your back.
2. To begin the movement, sweep your arms up and touch your palms at the top of your head. Be sure to continue dropping the shoulders down. Say, "I am tuned . . ."

3. Swan dive your arms out and over as you keep your back lengthened while you move through to position 2, resting the upper body over your legs. If you have tight hamstrings, keep your knees nice and soft. During this movement, say, ". . . in." *This is one rep.*
4. Move between position 1 and position 2, finding a nice flow. Find ease within the effort. Repeat 16 times.

Move 2: Side Lunge

Line 2: *I step into the flow*
With this mantra, you are stepping to both sides. Can you imagine that with each step you take, you are stepping into more ease, calm, and flow? While the lunge will work the legs, see if you can stay soft while doing it.

"I step into the flow"

1. Begin with your feet together, hands in prayer pose.
2. Keeping your toes pointing forward, step out to your right, bending your right leg but keeping your left leg straight. You are in a lateral lunge. Be sure that your right knee tracks right over your right toe. As you lunge, say, "I step into . . ."

3. Push off your right leg, bringing it back to the starting position. As you do so, say, ". . . the flow."
4. You will alternate sides, performing 8 lunges on each side for a total of 16.

Move 1: Prayer Fold

Line 3: *I have all that I need*
It's not uncommon to feel like the answers are outside of you or that you couldn't possibly have the resources you need in order to accomplish your goals. But I would like you to imagine that in this moment, you actually do have everything you could possibly need to take the very next step, whatever that may be. And then you have all you need to take the next step after that.

"I have all that I need"

1. Stand with your feet together and your hands by your side. Feel your heart lift as your shoulders melt down your back.
2. Sweep your arms up, and touch your palms at the top of your head. Be sure to continue dropping the shoulders. Say, "I have all . . ."

3. Swan dive your arms out and over as you keep your back lengthened while you move through to position 2, resting the upper body over your legs. If you have tight hamstrings, keep your knees nice and soft. During this movement, say, ". . . that I need." *This is one rep.*
4. Move between position 1 and position 2, finding a nice flow. Find ease within the effort. Repeat 16 times.

Move 2: Side Lunge

Line 4: *The rest I let go*
While using this mantra, take the time to let go of anything that is not in service of your highest good. This can be thoughts, feelings, or attitudes. As you perform the lunge this time, imagine all those things leaving your body, moving out through your feet.

"The rest I let go"

1. Begin with your feet together, hands in prayer pose.
2. Keeping your toes pointing forward, step out to your right, bending your right leg but keeping your left leg straight. You are in a lateral lunge. Be sure

that your right knee tracks right over your right toe. As you lunge, say, "The rest . . ."

3. Push off your right leg, bringing it back to the starting position. As you do so, say, ". . . I let go."
4. You will alternate sides, performing 8 lunges on each side for a total of 16.

Putting It All Together

Now you are going to put the *whole* thing together for 10 cycles. Simply alternate between Move 1 and Move 2. You should now be comfortable with the moves and have the full four-line mantra memorized. Do one move with one line at a time. So it will flow like this:

Move 1: Prayer Fold
Mantra: *I am tuned in*
(Pause; return to standing position so you can then prepare to lunge out to your right side.)

Move 2: Side Lunge
Mantra: *I step into the flow*
(You will only do one *lunge to your right side for this mantra and will be in the starting position to repeat Move 1.)*

Move 1: Prayer Fold
Mantra: *I have all that I need*
(Pause and slowly come up to the starting position so you are now ready to lunge to your left.)

Move 2: Side Lunge
Mantra: *The rest I let go*
(This time you will lunge out to your left, then return to the starting position to repeat the whole thing.)
This is one *cycle. You will repeat this whole cycle 10 times.*

CHAPTER 4

CHANGE YOUR BELIEFS

When I first started running workshops that combined movement and coaching, the groups were small and intimate. This allowed me to watch my students' transformations take place right before my eyes. I was so thrilled to see the impact of this work on my clients as they took ownership of their personal power and saw big changes in their lives. Some of them became more confident. Some found love. Others launched businesses or switched careers.

Before long, I thought, *Wouldn't it be great if I could reach more people and help them get similar results?* So I hired a business coach and studied the strategies that others had used to expand their reach. It became clear that creating an online program was the only way I could reach thousands of people, but I resisted—yes, that resistance problem we discussed in the last chapter.

I needed to find out why I couldn't bring myself to take my work online, so I used the strategies you'll learn in this chapter to dig deep and discover my beliefs about my business. What I found was that I believed people could only transform if I worked with them one-on-one. Even though I knew other coaches and teachers had been successful bringing results to long-distance clients, I held a belief that my message couldn't stand on its own unless I spoon-fed it to my clients while I stood over them. *That can't be the truth,* I told myself.

Then I dug even deeper and discovered another belief. If I wasn't directly in front of people, I believed I'd miss the instant feedback of those affirming head nods I got in class or one-on-one. With an online program, I'd have to put myself "out there" to be judged and potentially disliked by people who only saw me online and had never met me in person. It was scary, but I'm not sure what was scarier—the prospect of being disliked or the fact that my insecurities were holding me back.

Are you starting to see the conflict between my limiting beliefs and my desire to reach hundreds of thousands of people with my work? No wonder I wasn't experiencing business growth!

This conflict between beliefs and desires is a rampant problem. We get clear about our desires. We create a picture and a feeling of what it would be like to have what we want. We might even start to take action toward those desires. Yet despite our best efforts, they don't manifest. It starts to feel like life is against us, or maybe we just aren't supposed to have what we want. But the usual culprit is a limiting belief or two, and like so much of what stands in our way in life, beliefs are usually based on fear. The tragedy is that if we don't do the work to let go of those beliefs, our fondest wishes will never come true. That's an awful thought!

For example, I have a friend who really wants a relationship. She's an amazing woman with so much to offer, and she goes on plenty of dates. But inevitably, the men she falls for aren't available. They're involved with someone else, they don't want a committed relationship, or they don't live in the same city. Over and over, I've watched her fall passionately for men who can't give her what she wants.

She says she wants love. She takes action by putting herself out there. So why is she always attracted to the wrong men? While you could say she "just hasn't met the right guy yet," patterns like these point to beliefs that stand in the way.

My friend eventually discovered that she was deeply afraid of allowing her real self to be seen in a relationship. She believed her partner wouldn't like what he saw and would leave her. It's ironic but common—our fear of being alone leads to exactly that.

But like me, my friend needed to keep digging until she found another belief even deeper below the surface. What she discovered was a belief that she didn't deserve a man who would be open and available to her. She thought the men she met were the best she could do and that her standards had to be low in order to even have a chance at love. It boiled down to a belief that she wasn't worthy.

Why wasn't she meeting better men? Well, she probably was, but some part of her could feel intuitively that they were available, so there were no "sparks" with those men. Her beliefs were keeping her safe by keeping her alone. Better to have no luck than be rejected by somebody terrific, right? Ouch!

It took some work, but she was finally able to let go of that negative belief and create a relationship.

In many cases, we attract what we focus on, so if we have a limiting belief, we'll become magnetic to whatever reinforces that belief. Let's say you had a boss who insisted you work overtime every night without pay. So now you believe all bosses are likely to take advantage of you in this way. Unfortunately, this belief just might set you up for a pattern of bosses who do exactly that because you're attracting what you focus on out of fear—lousy bosses.

When we struggle with a pattern like this, it's easy to blame the world for not cooperating with our plans. But placing blame doesn't help us alter our future. Changing our beliefs, on the other hand, *does*.

Once I became aware of my limiting beliefs and understood why I was reluctant to take action toward expanding my business, I used the tools I'll share in this chapter to change my beliefs and move forward with my goals.

What about you? What desires did you uncover in Chapter 2 that you haven't been able to create? Have you noticed unwanted patterns playing out in your life? Do you have an idea of what beliefs might be standing in your way?

Negative beliefs are essentially negative thoughts. When we think them repeatedly, they become negative *mantras*. It's up to us to figure out what they are so that we can convert them into positive mantras.

That brings me to our mantra for this chapter, which will set the stage for you to transform your limiting beliefs:

I let go of the old
I'm creating something new
I choose my beliefs
It's easy to do!

Let's do a take two of that mantra because it's a deep and important one:

I let go of the old
I'm creating something new
I choose my beliefs
It's easy to do!

Next, let's examine some of your beliefs and see what you can bring to light that you didn't know before.

Journaling Exercise #5: Beliefs Exploration

Let's find out some of your limiting beliefs that are standing in the way of your desires. As always, be sure to write down your answers so that you can refer to them later.

You can use this series of questions to examine your beliefs about any desire you have, whether it's to develop inner strength, to begin to stand up for yourself, to lose weight, or to start a business. Answer them for one desire at a time, though.

1. Write down a desire you have that hasn't yet come true.

   Example #1: I want to get married.

   Example #2: I want to stand up for myself.

2. What actions have you taken toward manifesting this desire?

   Example #1: I've told friends I'm open to being set up, I've created profiles on dating apps, and I've been going on dates for several months.

   Example #2: I've started to write letters to the people I want to tell how I feel, and I'm in therapy.

3. What results have you gotten that are different from what you want? Describe them in detail, especially if you've seen a pattern.

    Example #1: I haven't had any relationships that lasted.

    Example #2: I haven't been able to speak up when others are unkind or unfair to me. I can only think of what to say afterward when I'm alone.

4. What are people related to this desire reflecting back to you? How are they showing up in your life?

    Example #1: I met a guy who has a girlfriend, another guy who was with me for a while but ultimately wasn't interested, and a guy who wanted a relationship but didn't turn me on. They're reflecting back to me that I have a belief that's holding me back from finding the right guy for me.

    Example #2: I seem to keep attracting people who are unkind or unfair to me, giving me lots of opportunities to speak up for myself. But I don't do it.

5. As a result of these issues, what do you believe about your desire?

    Example #1: I'm never going to find someone.

    Example #2: If I speak up, people won't like me, or they'll get mad at me. Then I'll have to deal with their anger, which scares me.

6. What do you believe about yourself as a result of not being able to manifest this desire?

    Example #1: I'm unlovable. I have too many issues for anyone to accept me as a partner.

    Example #2: I'm a coward.

7. What do you believe about others as a result of not being able to manifest this desire?

    Example #1: The only attractive men out there are unavailable, and the only men who are available are unattractive.

Example #2: A lot of people are mean, and they'll take advantage of you every chance they get.

8. What actions do you take or fail to take as a result of these limiting beliefs?

   Example #1: I quickly reject every man I meet.

   Example #2: No action. I don't stick up for myself.

Don't be disheartened by the results of this exercise. We're starting out by getting to the nasty stuff under the surface. Soon, you'll work on disengaging from these beliefs so that you can make way for your desires to come true. But let's jump-start that process by repeating our mantra:

I let go of the old
I'm creating something new
I choose my beliefs
It's easy to do!

Where Do Our Beliefs Come From?

Take a moment to imagine the following:

You're a little kid who keeps hearing a creaking sound in the basement of your family's house. You're sure there are monsters down there making the noises. What else could it be?

You go on with your everyday life as a child, but every now and then, you hear that creaking again, and the fear stops you in your tracks. It interrupts your playtime, keeps you from getting a good night's sleep (sometimes giving you nightmares), and makes you afraid to go down into the basement. If your mom asks you to grab something for her down there, you just can't do it. You get the shakes.

Well, many of your current limiting beliefs are like what's down in that basement. You don't see them. They're so far in your subconscious that you aren't aware of them. But they rattle around in your life, preventing you from taking action or getting what you want.

We form many of our beliefs when we're very young. Some beliefs result from what we were directly told or taught, and others are based on what we experienced and observed. For example, your parents might have told you the ocean is dangerous, and to this day, you're afraid of it. Someone might have said that you sing off key, and you interpreted that to mean that you should never sing again. Or you came to believe that marriage is painful because you watched your parents go through a divorce.

Unfortunately, when we're young, we observe the world through an uneducated lens so that many of our beliefs are based on misconceptions. If you think about it, I'll bet you can remember something you believed to be true as a kid that became silly to you when you got older. For example, one of my friends says she believed adults only slept because they wanted to, not because they had to. She has no idea how she came to believe such a thing. When she reached about age 12, she was surprised to find out that grown-ups actually *needed* to sleep.

That's a harmless belief, but many of the beliefs we develop as kids are far from harmless. These are our "core beliefs." We form them as we learn to understand life and the world around us, so our entire foundation is based on them. That's why they can be so tenacious. And they'll stay locked in our subconscious mind until we bring them into consciousness, which requires a trip down into the basement.

I know it can be scary even as an adult to go into our psyche's "basement," but don't worry, I'll be right there every step of the way. Just like we bravely stepped into the void, we're going to take out our flashlights, open the door, and head there together just to see what's causing the creaking noises. It may feel like some of your beliefs are monsters, but they aren't. We're simply going to find old beliefs that need to be replaced.

Once you've visited the basement, you'll likely have a better idea of what has held you back in your life. Whatever has kept you from achieving some of your goals, it isn't because you're "lazy," "incapable," or any other "I'm not enough" reason. Feel compassion for yourself. Remember that most of these beliefs were formed when you were too young to know any better. But left unchallenged, they'll continue to cause problems in your life. Shining a light on these deep beliefs will open up a whole new set of possibilities for you. Doesn't that sound worth a trip to the basement?

Journaling Exercise #6: Visit the Basement

1. Review the desires you wrote down in the last exercise or in Chapter 2, and choose the one that feels the most impossible, scary, or difficult to achieve.
2. Close your eyes and ask yourself: "Why can't I have this? What limiting beliefs might be preventing this desire from becoming my reality?" Write down as many beliefs as come to mind.

    Example: I want to lose 30 pounds.

    Possible limiting beliefs standing in my way:

    It will be too hard.

    I've lost weight before, and it always came back. So I'm sure it will again.

    My mom was always overweight. Therefore, I will be.

    Nobody will support me in my weight loss.

3. Now let's go deeper into the basement. Choose one of your beliefs, and ask yourself: "If my belief is true, then what?" Each time you answer, go deeper: "If this were true, what's the worst that could happen next? And what's the worst that could happen after that?"

    Example: I've lost weight before, and it always came back. So I'm sure it will again.

    If that were true, what's the worst that could happen?

I'd be right back where I started.

If that were true, what's the worst that could happen?

I'd have to start all over again.

If that were true, what's the worst that could happen?

I'd feel stuck.

If that were true, what's the worst that could happen?

I'd feel like a failure and not want to try again.

If that were true, what's the worst that could happen?

I'd be miserable and hate myself.

If that were true, what's the worst that could happen?

I'd never lose weight.

If that were true, what's the worst that could happen?

I wouldn't want to get out of bed in the morning or do anything at all.

If that were true, what's the worst that could happen?

I wouldn't have a social life and would spend all my time alone.

If that were true, what's the worst that could happen?

I'd be depressed and lonely and unloved.

If that were true, what's the worst that could happen?

I'd be all alone, and I'd want to die.

4. Remember I said it wasn't pretty down in the basement. But can you see that these beliefs are irrational? It's highly unlikely you'll be unloved and all alone just because you fail to lose weight.
5. Take a deep breath, and wrap your arms around yourself. You just did a brave thing and walked through your basement to the deepest level. Now let's continue so that you can begin to disengage from these beliefs and replace them with new ones.

The Irrationality of Limiting Beliefs

When I used to go through the exercise you just finished, no matter the belief I started with, I always ended up with the same fear: *I'm going to get cancer and die alone.*

It was always cancer. I'm sure this comes from my mother's cancer diagnosis when I was just a teenager. Even though my mother recovered, there was still a deep belief inside me that I would suffer the same fate and not make it. See what I mean when I say our beliefs are often irrational?

When my clients go through the previous exercise, they eventually get to beliefs like "I'm a failure. I'm a burden. I'm weird. I'm crazy. I'm not lovable. Something's wrong with me. I'm bad. I don't belong." If they go further still, they usually arrive at "I'll become homeless" or even further to "I'll die alone." Underneath nearly all our beliefs is the fear that we'll be dead and/or alone. But how likely is that in almost all circumstances?

We're all going to die eventually. We can't avoid it. And even if we find ourselves 100 percent alone at some point in our lives, it's usually short lived. There's almost always someone we can turn to, even if it's just someone on the other end of a hotline until we find someone more permanent and in person. There's almost always at least a tiny spark of light in the darkness.

The bottom line is: most of our core beliefs and fears are not based in reality and highly unlikely to ever happen. Once we see that they don't make sense, we can often chuckle about them, and their power is dissipated—like the monster in the basement who turns out to be funny looking.

We can then hold our inner child who formed these beliefs and reassure him/her that we're okay. The inner child within each of us never grows up, so we might have to offer that reassurance regularly, and maybe even on occasion for the rest of our lives. Just don't lose patience, and keep the reassurance coming. It's one of the ways you calm beliefs and fears so that you can move forward. You've no doubt heard the expression from Susan Jeffers, "Feel the fear and do it anyway." This is one of the ways you make that happen.

Some of my clients don't go down into the basement very far before they say about their fearful beliefs, "If that were true, I'd figure it out. I'd find a way to make it work." I'll bet that's what you'd do, too, especially if you discovered just how irrational your core beliefs truly were.

Let's find out right now if some of your beliefs are irrational and untrue.

Journaling Exercise #7: The Coat of Your Beliefs

- Choose one of the beliefs you unearthed in one of the other two exercises.

    Example: I'm a failure.

- Ask yourself: Can I know 100 percent that this belief is true?

    Example: No, I can't know 100 percent that I'm a failure. In fact, I can list a lot of times I was successful.

    Think of how silly it is to act based on a belief that you don't even know to be true!

- Imagine that this belief is a coat. Put on this coat and pretend you're walking around your home with it on. Close your eyes, and see yourself walking into the kitchen, into the bathroom, into the bedroom, and then outside. Imagine that you're wearing this coat when you're out with friends or spending time with loved ones. The truth is that you *are* wearing this coat when you're doing all of these activities. Write down how this coat makes you feel. Does it make you feel sad and depressed?

    Example: When I wear the coat of failure, I feel terrible. I feel like I have no right to be in the world and like no one should want to spend time with me. It's awful!

- Next, think about how you act in the world when you feel like this. Write down what you do as a result of this coat you wear.

  Example: I get quiet and shy, hiding my humor and ideas. I don't try new things. I apologize for being myself and taking up space. I let others walk all over me because I feel like they're successful, and I'm not. Therefore, they deserve more than I do.

- Take your limiting belief and turn it on its head. This is a new mantra for you. It doesn't matter if you don't believe it right away.

  Example: I'm a successful person.

- Now try on the coat of your new belief, and imagine walking around wearing this one. How does it make you feel to wear this coat in your home and around other people?

  Example: Wearing the coat of success, I feel like I can be myself around other people. I can crack jokes and tell them what I think. I feel like I can step into the life I'm supposed to have.

- If you wear this new coat all the time, what do you think you could accomplish?

  Example: I could be successful in business and in relationships. I'd have the confidence I've lacked all my life because I'd know that I'm worthy and capable.

- While we do have a mantra for this chapter, you can use the mantra you create here with the movement, if you prefer. That will help you solidify your new belief into your bones and your muscles and your heart. It may take some time to override your old belief, but if you keep moving the mantra, giving it the full power of all your energy, physically and emotionally, you'll begin to have the courage to take new action. As you experience positive results from those actions, you'll take yet more actions that will solidify your new truth.

- Do this exercise for as many beliefs as you wish!
- If you find that one of your beliefs causes you to really shake in your shoes, try writing a letter to your inner child, quelling his/her fears. You could write something like, *"Little one, I know you've been through a lot, and I understand why you believe you're a failure. But you aren't, and here's why. Let's remember all the times you were successful. [List your successes throughout life, starting from a young age.] You learned to walk! You learned to talk! You graduated elementary school and high school! [Keep going.] But look, it's important to try new things, and sometimes, we don't perform perfectly the first time. We have to keep trying. That's true for everybody. So remember that I'm here to protect you, and we can take the risk without suffering great harm. We aren't going to end up alone. People aren't going to stop loving us. In fact, who wants anyone to be perfect, really? And who's worth keeping around if they stop loving us for not being perfect? Know that I love you and will watch over you as we start to take more risks and wear the coat of success."*

Your Subconscious Mind

My friend and manifesting consultant Catherine Collautt, Ph.D., has written a lot about the power of the subconscious mind and how our beliefs cause us to be in automatic mode unless and until we harness its power. Catherine says to think of your subconscious as a computer. "It's going to take its programming and run with it; it's your job to make sure that its programming is in functional, if not optimal, alignment with your goals by programming, re-programming and de-bugging, at regular intervals. And in concert with your goals—as they change, as new ones arise, and so on."

In other words, we have to learn how to master our subconscious. "Mastery involves, first taking up our position of power in relation to our subconscious, not by trying to outdo it or by doing without it; but by realizing it's our job to clean up the programming and directions we have (wittingly or unwittingly) given our blessed processing powerhouse," Catherine stresses. "When you make your subconscious a friend, and even a best friend, the process of . . . materializing your dreams and desires, changes entirely. . . . Remember there is no antagonism when it comes to your subconscious. Its power is the asset not the obstacle. Your subconscious is on your side; it wants to be on your side. Even when it looks like it's totally against you. As the dedicated and indefatigable employee that it is, it's probably just working on a mission you gave it and forgot about, years ago."

As we replace limiting beliefs with new ones, we reprogram the computer that is our subconscious and turn it into a best friend that works with us to create the sweet life we want. That's what moving the mantras will do for you. Let's get to it!

MANTRA IN MOTION #3

Let's reprogram that inner computer and set a new standard with your beliefs movement sequence. You're no longer wearing the coat of the old. With each move, you are in command! You expand and choose the beliefs that will bring you a sweeter life.

Your Beliefs Mantra
I let go of the old
I'm creating something new
I choose my beliefs
It's easy to do!

Move 1: Upper Body Release in a Plié Squat

Line 1: *I let go of the old*

You identified several beliefs that you would like to transform. Which ones are you ready to let go of? Letting go can be cathartic, so get ready to turn up the heat!

"I let go of the old"

1. Bring your legs to a plié squat position, and bend your arms so your hands come in toward your chest. It should feel like you are holding a large, soft ball in your hands. This imagery will help you keep the energy alive in your hands.
2. Extend your arms out straight while keeping the legs in a plié squat.
3. Pump your arms in and out at a pace that is comfortable for you. Don't worry about how many times they go in and out, just find a rhythm that works and remember to bring the energy to this. Your legs will naturally bounce a little.
4. As you pump your arms, say the mantra, "I let go of the old!" (Of course, you will say, "1" after you say the mantra in order to count the reps.) Repeat the mantra 16 times, though the number of times you extend your arms will be determined by your speed. Your objective is to get your heart rate up on this a little, so don't be afraid to really let it go!

Move 2: Chair Pose Legs, Fast Circle of the Arms

Line 2: *I'm creating something new*

Again, you're going to get your energy going with this move and mantra. You can even think of yourself as the "Little Engine that Could." In order to create something new, you have to put a little "oomph" behind your feelings, thoughts, heart, and body. Bring to mind what you're creating today, this week, and this month. You can do it!

"I'm creating something new"

1. Bring your feet together and sit down in a chair pose. Sit as low as you can.
2. Bring your arms into the position shown in the illustration and start to circle the arms away from you, as fast as you can.
3. Get those arms going, and whatever you do, don't stop. Find your own rhythm and say the mantra, "I'm creating something new."
4. You will be counting the number of times you say the mantra, but it doesn't matter how many circles of the arms you make. Repeat the mantra 16 times.

Move 1: Upper Body Release in a Plié Squat

Line 3: *I choose my beliefs*

As you know, your beliefs are a thought that you think over and over. They get ingrained in your mind like a groove in an old vinyl record. The good news is that you get to choose new ones that empower and support you. Perhaps you want to bring to mind one of your new beliefs as you do this move and mantra. Hold it in your mind's eye as you continue to keep your energy vibrant and alive!

"I choose my beliefs"

1. Bring your legs to a plié squat position; bend your arms so your hands come in toward your chest. Again, imagine that large, soft ball in your hands.
2. Extend your arms out straight while keeping the legs in a plié squat.
3. Pump your arms in and out at a pace that seems comfortable for you. Don't worry about how many times they go in and out; just find a rhythm that works and remember to bring the energy to this. Your legs will naturally bounce a little.

4. As you pump your arms, say the mantra, "I choose my beliefs!" (Of course, you will say, "1" after you say the mantra in order to count the reps.) You will repeat the mantra 16 times; the number of times you extend the arms will be determined by your speed.

Move 2: Chair Pose Legs, Fast Circle of the Arms

Line 4: *It's easy to do*

We often think it's difficult to change from within. But I invite you to play with the idea that what you used to think was hard is now easy to do. What does it feel like to just nod your head and say, "Yes, it's easy"? You can apply this mantra to many areas of your life!

"It's easy to do"

1. Bring your feet together and sit down in a chair pose. Sit as low as you can.
2. Bring your arms to the position shown in the illustration and start to circle the arms away from you as fast as you can.

3. Get those arms going, and whatever you do, don't stop. Find some ease inside the effort and say the mantra, "It's easy to do."
4. You will be counting the number of times you say the mantra, but it doesn't matter how many circles of the arms you make. Repeat the mantra 16 times.

Putting It All Together

Remember that you can always join me in the video for more direction.

Now you're going to put the whole cycle together for 10 cycles. Alternate between Move 1 and Move 2. Do one move with one line at a time, so it will flow like this:

Move 1: Upper Body Release in a Plié Squat
Mantra: *I let go of the old*
(Push your arms out as many times as you can while saying the mantra. When you complete it, jump or bring your feet together for the next move.)

Move 2: Chair Pose Legs, Fast Circle of the Arms
Mantra: *I'm creating something new*
(Circle your arms as fast as you can while you say the mantra. When you are done, step or jump out to the plié squat position.)

Move 1: Upper Body Release in a Plié Squat
Mantra: *I choose my beliefs*
(Same as above, doing as many as you can while saying the mantra one time. Then jump or bring your feet together for the next move.)

Move 2: Chair Pose Legs, Fast Circle of the Arms
Mantra: *It's easy to do*
(Circle your arms quickly, say the mantra, and jump or step out to the next move.)
This is one *cycle. You will repeat this whole cycle 10 times.*

TAKE INSPIRED ACTION

After I worked through the old beliefs that were holding me back, I was ready to expand my business and reach more people. Don't get me wrong—I was still scared. But my inner work meant I was just no longer being driven by those limiting beliefs.

In order to move beyond the New York City fitness and wellness market, I knew that creating video content was the way to go. Putting the videos online would allow people from across the world to learn about my work in the comfort of their own homes.

But I wanted even more than that. I wanted to create a spectacular program so that people could log on and feel like they were in a safe, beautiful space, as though they were working directly with me.

While a few people were having success with online programs, those kinds of videos hadn't yet hit the mainstream. So there weren't many resources to help me learn how to do it. I was pretty much on my own to figure it out. Plus, I didn't know the first thing about producing fitness videos—the cameras, lights, sound, studio space, or any other aspect of it.

Then there was the financial perspective. The investment in my dream would not come cheap. Yes, my coaching business was growing, but it was slow growth. So I didn't have much money to spare. Would I be able to make that money back, or would it be a total wash and a waste of time that I'd live to regret?

I battled so many "what if" thoughts. *What if this is a flop? What if nobody wants to buy it? What if I come across as unlikeable or unintelligent?* What if, what if, what if . . .

But this dream was so deeply connected to my inner desires and my core values that I knew I had to figure out how to do it. I began slowly, reaching out to people I knew in production. I looked for affordable places I could shoot. I investigated what kind of music I needed. I made lists and lists . . . and more lists.

Much of the information I learned was completely new to me. But little by little, I found myself with a full production crew, a camera crew, a sound mixer, and dates on the calendar to shoot my videos.

I spent hours putting together the right movements with mantras and rehearsing the workouts with my students. When it came time to shoot the videos, it was the culmination of both the inner work I had done on my beliefs and the outer work—the actions—I had taken. It was a remarkable day.

But that was still only the beginning of the process. I had yet to create the online portal and content. There were many days I had no idea what I was doing or how it would turn out, including frustrating hours with my editor as we tried to fix problems with the videos that weren't done properly during the shoot. Sometimes I felt overwhelmed and exhausted, but I continued to put one foot in front of the other until I was finished.

And here's what happened: I've been able to reach people in more than 135 countries in the world. It brought me partners, press, and people who allowed me to do exactly what I'd been burning to do—expand. I took *inspired action to bring this dream to life.*

Sometimes, we take action in order to *make* something happen. And sometimes we take *inspired action* to move with the energy that's already in motion. The key is to recognize when you're trying to force or push versus working with inspiration, excitement, and flow.

Inspired action usually looks like this:

1. You get an idea or impulse to do something that comes to you naturally, easily, and at an unexpected moment. (Whenever these ideas enter your mind, be sure to write them down so that you remember them.)

2. The action steps simply *feel* right, even if they don't always make logical sense. Even if the path isn't 100 percent clear to you yet.
3. When you start to take the action, you feel energized.
4. You're able to make progress quickly, and you maximize your time.
5. You don't feel fully in control, but you feel as though there's a helping hand moving you along.
6. You enjoy the tasks, even if your fear voice is still present.

When you take action from your ego or fear, it usually looks like this:

7. You spend a lot of time trying to analyze what actions to take. You might spend days or weeks struggling to take a step forward because you are overanalyzing every choice.
8. You talk and talk about what you're *going* to do, throwing in a few complaints to your friends or your spouse, but you find it difficult to get started.
9. When you do finally take action, you feel tired and depleted. The actions you take feel like "work," and you have to make yourself move toward your goal.
10. You find yourself continuously stopped by roadblocks. There's no flow or forward movement.
11. You feel like you have to *make* it happen and push your way there.

How do you move yourself into a space of inspired action? My initial advice is to revisit your desires, core values, and personal brand of resistance (Journaling Exercises #1, #2, and #3). Then ask: Am I truly moving in the direction I want or in the direction I *think* I *should*?

Inspired action should feel like playing. You should find that you want to take the steps toward your goal regardless of the end result. That brings me to our mantra for this chapter:

I am taking action
I have love in my soul
No worries, no regrets
I am ready to go!

Let's repeat it again:

I am taking action
I have love in my soul
No worries, no regrets
I am ready to go!

Letter to the Universe

Years before I got married, I felt unsettled about a previous long-term relationship. While I was already dating someone new, I couldn't seem to get my ex out of my mind. I began to wonder if I should take action on that feeling. Then my longtime coach and friend Julie-Anne Lee Kinney shared a profound journaling exercise that helped me make my decision and discover whether my action would be forced or inspired.

For the exercise, I sat down and wrote a "letter to the Universe," asking what I should do. Should I reach out to him? Should I let him go?

Then I sat down to write a letter to myself *from* the Universe. The only message I got was, "Be patient. Wait and see. Let it unfold." It was frustrating. Did that mean I should wait and see if he would come back into my life? In the moment, it didn't feel like a very action-oriented answer, but maybe patience was an action that meant simply keeping my eyes and ears open. So that's what I did.

Later that night, I went for a walk in my neighborhood, which also happened to be my ex's neighborhood. Suddenly, I saw someone walking a familiar-looking dog.

I approached her and said, "Is that Wookie?"

Wookie was my ex-boyfriend's dog.

"Yes, it is. Are you Erin?" she asked.

I'd never seen this woman before, so I couldn't believe she knew who I was. She proceeded to tell me that she was my ex-boyfriend's new girlfriend.

I was in shock. I had no idea he was dating someone new, and finding out was a bit painful. But I also knew this run-in was my follow-up answer from the Universe. It was telling me, "It's time to let go of him." I did my best to smile and be gracious to his new girlfriend, even though I was burning inside.

It would have been nice to get the "let him go" message before I had to experience the pain of running into the new girlfriend. But I believe it unfolded for my highest good. Had I not seen her, I might not have trusted a clear "let it go" message in my Letter from the Universe. I think that I needed that extra and somewhat firm kick in the tush.

Since that experience, I've used the Letter to the Universe as a magic tool whenever I feel stuck or feel I'm pushing myself toward a goal from a place of ego or fear. It's one of the best ways I know for figuring out if my desired action is inspired and determining my best next step. You can call it a Letter to Life, to God, or to My Inner Self. It doesn't really matter as long as you feel connected to it.

I admit that sometimes the answers don't make sense right away. I have gotten messages like, "You're doing great. Don't do anything yet." Or I'm "told" something that seems unrelated to my question, such as "Call your friend Will," when the problem has nothing to do with him (or so I think). But if I follow through on whatever comes through, the dots always eventually connect. And I usually at least receive my very next step, which is what leads to the unfolding of the rest of the answer.

Here are two Letters *to* the Universe and Letters *from* the Universe to give you an idea of what they might look like:

1. Dear Universe: I'm not sure if I should let go of the Thursday class I'm teaching. It's giving me a little anxiety, but I'm not totally ready to give it up. What's my next step? Love, Erin

Dear Erin: I think you can let it go. I'm cooking up something else that I think you're going to enjoy more. But you have to trust me and be open to what's coming. Love, The Universe

2. Dear Universe: I'm dating someone new. I know he likes me a lot, but I'm not sure how I feel about him. Can I get some clarity on what I should do next with the relationship? Love, Erin

   Dear Erin: Let him love you for right now. It's what he really wants to do. Then see what happens from there. We can figure the rest out as we go. Love, The Universe

Of course, your letters can be as long or detailed as you like, and you might want to write them frequently. That's what my client Nancy does. She even addresses her letters *to* the Universe to her work email address, where she feels more organized and less chaotic. Her letters *from* the Universe are sent from work to her home email address.

Nancy's life at home has been challenging, to say the least. She and her husband have a child with chronic fatigue syndrome. Taking care of their daughter often puts stress on both of them as they try to support her as best they can. At the same time, Nancy has a desire to return to her greatest love and passion—music. She wants to start a choir and spend more time playing piano, singing, and immersing herself in music. But it has been difficult to balance her marriage, her daughter, and her own passions. Writing letters to and from the Universe helped her clarify the action steps she needed to take to feel more balanced and move forward with her dreams.

"The idea that the response is from the 'all-seeing, all-knowing Universe' makes it so powerful that for a while, I was writing these letters every day," Nancy says. "Often, the Universe successfully consoles me or gives me new ideas."

Like Nancy, I recommend using this tool whenever you need guidance, clarity, direction, or inspiration to take action in any area of your life, from love to career.

Journaling Exercise #8: Your Own Letters to and from the Universe

What's troubling you? Where do you need clarity about an action you're considering? Carve out at least 15 minutes to sit down and write your letters.

1. Grab your journal (I prefer to write it by hand, but you can type it on a computer or handheld device), and sit down with a very specific question in mind. Start your letter with "Dear Universe," and don't hold back. Write down how you feel, what you want to know, and what you're concerned about.
2. Write the letter back to yourself from the Universe. You can attempt to write it immediately, or you may wish to wait until later that night or the next day. Allow the pen to flow without thinking about what you're writing. This is how you can bypass your conscious mind and surprise yourself. If nothing comes, or if you don't understand what the Universe has to say to you, wait a bit. Say out loud, "I'm open to receiving the answer in whatever form you want to give it to me." Then keep your eyes and ears open. You just might find your clarity around the corner, walking your ex-boyfriend's dog! Whatever and however the information comes to you, trust that even if it's still not 100 percent clear, it's for your highest good and that all will be clearer in due time.

Baby Steps

When I was a teenager, my mom used to say, "Erin, you're running around like a chicken with its head cut off!" I hated that observation, but she was probably right. What she meant was that I was always in a stage of *doing, doing, doing.* I moved from one activity to the next without pausing or bothering to organize my actions.

I continued this pattern into my 20s as I tried to tackle any and every project that came my way. I was hungry to accomplish everything I possibly could, so I loaded my list with "to-dos." What I didn't realize was that my inner dialogue said, *There's never enough time. I'll never get it all done.* It kept me in a constant state of stress.

Then, one day, I was in Vermont with a friend, visiting her uncle, who was working on a vintage car from the 1940s in his garage. Part of the car was open, and there were wires everywhere. It was a big mess.

"My goal is to get the car running again," he told us.

"Wow," I said, "how are you doing to accomplish that with these pieces all over the place?" I just couldn't imagine that the car would ever be a functioning machine again.

"One wire at a time," he answered.

I immediately recognized that what he said was the perfect metaphor for getting past fear, being overwhelmed, and overcoming paralysis. The comment has stayed with me ever since. It's one of the key ways I calm myself down when I feel there's too much to do and not enough time to do it. I take baby steps, breaking down my tasks into the smallest possible increments of action—one wire at a time. This is how I feel the fear and do it anyway.

Here's a simple example of how I used this strategy. I once wanted to transfer a video from a tape (yes, the old-fashioned kind) to a DVD, borrowing a friend's video camera to accomplish the task. But because I didn't have any idea how to do it, I kept putting it off. The camera sat in the corner of my apartment for months until my friend said, "Hey, Erin, where's my camera?" Finally, I made myself a to-do list that included every single, even obvious, increment of the task:

1. Take the video camera out of the corner.
2. Unzip the camera case.
3. Remove the camera.
4. Plug the cord into the back of the camera.

Etc.

When I broke it down into these oversimplified, tiny, manageable steps, the chore felt much less intimidating. I could even finish just a few of the steps one day and move on to more steps the next day.

This tactic works well for many actions that feel daunting. Maybe you need to send a business pitch email or write about a difficult subject to a significant other, friend, or family member. Again, try breaking it down into these small steps:

1. Sit down at the computer. *That isn't scary, is it?*
2. Open the computer. *Still not scary.*
3. Turn on the computer. *Not scary.*
4. Click Compose Message. *Maybe a little bit scarier, but still not so frightening because you haven't sent anything.*
5. Write the message. *This is a bit scarier, but remember that you still haven't sent it!*
6. Click Send. *This is truly the scariest part of the task, and it takes all of two seconds.*

The most frightening part of this particular task is so short that it's almost laughable! Now, I know full well that those two seconds can be very scary, but think of it this way: you only need two seconds of insane, outrageous courage. Just two seconds of it! We'll talk more about building your courage "muscles" later. Right now, let's stay focused on creating an action plan.

So, what about big projects with a long list of to-dos? Here's what I do: every year, in order to determine my best plan of inspired action for my business, I sit down and think about my goals and desires for the year. For me, this means financial goals as well as personal, creative goals.

Then I ask myself, "What are all the possible ways in which I *might* reach these goals from where I sit right now?" Next, I do a big brain dump, writing down anything and everything that might be interesting for me to do with my team to get to those goals, whether it's to create a new product or come up with a different way to sell an existing product. I write down suggestions I've gotten from others, what clients have said they want, and even what I've seen competitors doing, in case that sparks a new idea. I also write down the kinds of partnerships I'd like to create and names of people I might like to work with.

You can do this same kind of brain dump for your career desires, body desires, financial desires, home desires, and even relationship desires. And in a moment, that's exactly what we're going to do.

But for now let's revisit our mantra:

I am taking action
I have love in my soul
No worries, no regrets
I am ready to go!

Which Came First—
the Confidence or the Action?

The most important aspect of this process is simply taking action. Even if you worry that your action isn't as "inspired" as you'd like it to be, never use anything in this chapter as an excuse to beat yourself up or compare yourself to anyone else.

Learning new skills can take time and can be clunky along the way. We often see other people accomplishing their goals and think, *Wow, she's so confident*, or *I wish I could be a go-getter like him!* We believe we have to create more confidence within ourselves in order to be able to take the actions. But the only way to gain more confidence is to do what we're afraid to do—to take action. It's almost impossible to have confidence about something we've never tried before.

So if you're working toward a goal that makes you shake in your shoes or sends you into that awful state of being overwhelmed, even if you only manage steps one and two the first day, applaud yourself. There's nobility in your action, even if you feel like you're moving forward at a snail's pace. Whatever speed you walk in, if it's in the direction of your goal, it's progress, and I'm proud of you for it!

Journaling Exercise #9: Create Your Plan of Inspired Action

People often get tripped up when trying to create an action plan because they think it needs to be perfect. So I'm going to walk you through your own plan, even if you feel you have no clue how to accomplish your goal. You'll soon see that it's a lot less intimidating than you think!

We'll start by choosing a goal, doing a brain dump, and choosing the project(s) to focus on, and then we'll break down the tasks into baby steps. Give yourself 30 minutes for this journaling exercise.

1. Revisit your Dig for Gold and Set Your Vision 12-month list (p. 25), and choose a dream you want to accomplish. It can be for any aspect of your life. Maybe you want to expand your business or look for a new job or career. Maybe you want to attract a new romantic partner into your life.
2. Start your brain dump by asking yourself: "What are all the different ways to go about creating this in my life?" Be aware that your mind might jump ahead to, "But I don't know how to do that!" or "I don't have the resources for that!" Don't worry about those issues for now. Just write down every possible idea that comes to mind. Think about how someone else might go about accomplishing this goal. Keep going until you're truly out of ideas. It's sort of like a "brain dump dream list."

    Example: Let's say this is the year you really desire to love your body, feel energized on a daily basis, and finally feel confident every time you get dressed in the morning. Think about what might help you get there. Here is what your brain dump might look like:

- Find a movement program that's fun and lights me up.
- Find an accountability partner who will inspire me to move my body regularly.
- Learn to cook healthy meals.
- Drink more water.
- Learn how to plan my meals for the week.
- Go through my closet and get rid of any clothes that make me feel frumpy.
- Hire a personal shopper or enlist a friend to help me find clothes that are right for my body.
- Move my body with self-love mantras.
- Deepen my spiritual practice so that I feel less frazzled and more connected to myself.
- Read books on positive body image.

3. Review your brain dump and the potential ways of accomplishing your goal. Ask yourself these questions, and write down your answers:
    - Which of these ideas are in alignment with my core values?
    - Which of them "light me up" and sound fun?
    - Which of them feel like they'd truly move me closer to my dream?
    - Do any of these feel like heavy or hard work? Which of these would I dread trying to execute?

    Based on your answers, choose three actions/ideas/projects that sound like the most fun and most aligned with your core values. You can always pick more later, but three is a manageable number for starters.

4. Allow yourself to *feel* your way into each of these projects. Close your eyes, and imagine working on each one. How does it feel in your bones and in your heart? Yes, some might be more time-consuming than others, but anything worthwhile

is worth the effort. For each of the three actions/ideas/projects, ask yourself these questions:

- If I were to spend the next few months working on this project, would I feel accomplished at the end of it?
- Would I feel proud?
- Would I enjoy it?
- Would I be closer to or possibly have achieved my desires?

5. Based on your answers, choose one of your actions/ideas/projects to start, and let's create your Master Project List. You can do this online or in your journal. Give your Master Project any name you like, but make it a fun one! Let's say you chose to find a movement plan that lights you up. You could call it "Ready to Move!"
6. Now that you have the name of your Master Project, do another brain dump of all the action items you think it would take to accomplish this project. For each action, ask yourself if it needs further breaking down. *Example: "Research gyms in my area" may require several small actions like "Research online," "Visit gyms in my neighborhood," and "Ask Mary Ann what her favorite way to move is."*
7. After you've written all the actions down, review them to see if they fall into different categories. If so, organize them based on these categories. *Example: If I'm going to create a new product for my business, I know that there will be actions to take for marketing, design, production, financials, etc. I want to file each action under its proper category to help me conserve time when I'm ready to move the ball forward.*

    Here's another example: *What if your desire is to find a new job? Your categories might be research, self-care and reflection, and networking/outreach.* Get the idea? Then, for each action, treat it as though you're giving the assignment to a first grader, and break it down into the smallest steps you can possibly make, such as:

Self-care and reflection:

- *Make a list of the pros and cons for leaving my current job.*
- *Visualize what my ideal day would look like, including going to a new job. Have coffee with Sara and ask her about how she found the job she loves.*
- *Do movements and mantras so that I am in alignment with my desires and core values.*
- *Appreciate the job I have today.*
- *Pray for guidance and direction.*
- *Tell five people I know that I am looking for a new job.*

8. Next to each step, estimate how long you think it will take to accomplish that step—two seconds, five minutes, a half hour? This will prevent you from becoming overwhelmed by the amount of time it will take to achieve your goal. Add in a little cushion of time since most actions take us longer than we anticipate. Here are a couple of examples of what that might look like:
   - *Make a list of the pros and cons for leaving my current job—20 minutes.*
   - *Visualize what my ideal day would look like, including going to a new job—10 minutes daily.*
9. Circle the scariest step on your list. That's the step you'll focus on when using the mantra from this chapter. When you're ready to take action on this step, go to page 102 to do the movements as you say your mantra. Nine times out of ten, this helps my clients finish that scariest step! And don't forget that I'm here with you all the way!

Here's our mantra again to keep you inspired!

I am taking action
I have love in my soul
No worries, no regrets
I am ready to go!

Trust That Your Actions Will Move You Forward

Before we move on, I want to share something profound that I learned when I created the Shrink Session videos. Please lean in because this one is especially important!

At the end of the very arduous shoot schedule for the videos, I stood in the room, looking at the crew and feeling exhausted. But I was so incredibly proud of what we'd achieved. Simply by following through and taking inspired action on my desire, I grew my self-confidence. I was actually a new person standing on an unexplored precipice of the mountain of life.

From this *new* perspective, I had a vision of what I wanted to do next—even though it was before I'd sold even one product from the video launch. So the process wasn't about the money or the accolades. It was about what I gained as a person and who I became because I took inspired action. The *true* gifts of moving forward were increased self-confidence and self-esteem. No one could take those away from me, even if my videos ended up being a bust.

The steps that we take aren't always about the tangible result they'll create. They're often about the lessons we learn, the perspectives we gain, and the confidence we build each time we develop new skills.

Don't measure your success based on some quantifiable outcome. Measure it based on what you develop within yourself, and give yourself credit for every single baby step you take. Sometimes my clients question whether taking one baby step toward what they want will make a difference at all. They wonder if going to the gym *one* time will change anything. They think simply registering for an online dating app is pointless. They question whether or not going out for a walk will really have an impact on the creative project they're stuck on.

But I want you to think of these small actions as more than just baby steps. They're offerings to Life, the Universe, or whatever you want to call it. You're raising your hand, extending your hand up and saying, "Life, I'm really interested in making this dream come true. I may not have all the answers. I may not know where all of this is going, but I'm committed to my dream." Then you take one little action as a way of proving to life that you're serious.

When you take a step toward life—even a miniscule baby step—life will take a step toward you. It's energy meeting like energy. Taking action isn't just about getting stuff done. It's more about being generous with yourself—generous with your time, talent, and ideas.

Take your baby steps. Then watch what happens. This is usually when synchronicity starts to come into play. Each little action allows Life to open up for you just a little bit more.

As *The Alchemist* author Paulo Coelho once said, "When someone makes a decision, he is really diving into a strong current that will carry him to places he had never dreamed of when he first made the decision." Let's move your mantras and get you flowing with the strong current toward the life you desire.

MANTRA IN MOTION #4

One of the most inspired actions you can take is movement with your mantra! So take action right this minute as a way of inspiring yourself to take even more actions that will move you toward your goals. No worries, no regrets. Feel the love in your soul as you spend just five minutes to make positive changes happen!

Your Inspired Action Mantra
I am taking action
I have love in my soul
No worries, no regrets
I am ready to go!

Move 1: Single Arm Punches

Line 1: *I am taking action*
It's time to get movin'! Get ready to declare that today is the day you're going to take one step forward—or maybe several steps. Imagine that you're knocking your inner obstacles out of the way. This is a great workout to do along with me in the video.

"I am taking action"

1. Start with your legs about hips' distance apart, keeping the knees soft. Bring your arms up to the ready position as seen in the illustration.
2. Twisting from your center, extend one arm at a time into a straight arm punch. Be sure to really reach the arm nice and long while keep the other arm in that ready position.

3. Switch arms and start to find a nice rhythm of these single punches.
4. You will be more focused on saying and counting the mantra than you will be about how many punches you should do. Allow yourself to let loose with the punches, building more confidence with each one. Say, "I am taking action" once you find a good rhythm. Repeat the mantra 16 times.

Move 2: Chair Pose Rising

Line 2: *I have love in my soul*
Sometimes we take action out of fear. But today, I want you to take action from a place of love. It's the most powerful force for accomplishing goals. When you move forward with love in your heart and soul, you'll easily find that sense of flow we've been talking about.

"I have love in my soul"

1. Starting with your feet together, bend your knees as if sitting in a chair, and swing your arms behind you. Sit down as low as you can. Say, "I have love in my . . ."
2. Straighten your legs, and swing your arms up over your head. Be sure to relax your shoulders. On the way up, say, ". . . soul." *This is one rep.*
3. Find a gentle flow between these two positions. Repeat this movement and mantra 16 times.

Move 1: Single Arm Punches

Line 3: *No worries, no regrets*
Sometimes I take action and then second-guess myself, wondering if I did the right thing. I have to remind myself that all action is progress. Since we're going for progress, not perfection, we say, "No worries, no regrets." Remember that when you give your best, your best gets better.

"No worries, no regrets"

1. Stand with your legs about hips' distance apart, keeping the knees soft. Bring your arms up to the ready position as seen in the illustration.

2. Twisting from your center, extend one arm at a time into a straight arm punch. Be sure to really reach the arm nice and long while keeping the other arm in that ready position.
3. Switch arms and find a nice rhythm of these single punches.
4. Focus on saying and counting the mantra and not on how many punches you do. Allow yourself to let go of any worries or regrets with every twist and punch, building more confidence with each one. Say, "No worries, no regrets" once you find a good rhythm. Repeat the mantra 16 times.

Move 2: Chair Pose Rising

Line 4: *I am ready to go*
Before you begin this one, I invite you to nod your head yes and silently say to yourself, "I'm ready." See what it feels like to affirm that you already have what you need in this moment to move forward. Now let's put this into action.

"I am ready to go"

1. Starting with your feet together, bend your knees as if sitting in a chair, and swing your arms behind you. Sit down as low as you can. Say, "I am ready to . . ."
2. Straighten your legs, and swing your arms up over your head. Be sure to relax your shoulders. On the way up, say, ". . . go." As you rise, feel as though you're almost lifting off. *This is one rep.*
3. Find a gentle flow between these two positions. Repeat this movement and mantra 16 times.

Putting It All Together

Now you're going to put the whole cycle together for 10 cycles. Alternate between Move 1 and Move 2. Do one move with one line at a time, so it will flow like this:

Move 1: Single Arm Punches
Mantra: *I am taking action*
(Once you get your arms going, say the mantra out loud one time and think it to yourself one time before moving on to the next move. Once you've done that, simply bring your feet together in preparation for Chair Pose Rising.)

Move 2: Chair Pose Rising
Mantra: *I have love in my soul*
(Do this move two times—one time saying the mantra out loud and the next time just thinking it. Then step your feet back out to prepare for the Single Arm Punches.)

Move 1: Single Arm Punches
Mantra: *No worries, no regrets*

(Once you get your arms going, say the mantra one time out loud and think it to yourself the second time. Then bring your feet together to do another Chair Pose Rising.)

Move 2: Chair Pose Rising
Mantra: *I am ready to go*
(Repeat this movement and mantra two times. You will say it out loud once and then think it to yourself the second time.)
This is one *cycle. You will repeat this whole cycle 10 times.*

CHAPTER 6

CULTIVATE COURAGE

My heart was racing, my mouth was dry, pools of sweat formed in my palms, and butterflies were swarming in my stomach.

What do you assume I was feeling? If you're quick to answer "fear," you're probably in the majority. When you feel those same physical symptoms, do you immediately think, *Oh my gosh, I'm so scared*?

Even Bruce Springsteen has the same physiological reaction before he walks up to the microphone. The difference is that he doesn't label those symptoms as "fear." No, not the Boss! To him, these feelings are his signal that it's time to run right out there and rock 'n' roll. He calls it "excitement."

I'll bet those moments when you've felt excited, your body reacted in a similar way. In fact, scientists at Harvard University conducted a study that showed people perform better when they label those symptoms as excitement rather than fear. It's all in the interpretation!

One of my acting teachers, Josh Pais, has a father who is a physicist, so he often talked about how the molecules in our bodies bounce around when we're both excited and afraid. He used to say, "Party with your fear" as a way of reframing all that molecule bouncing. He'd ask us to think of the physiological symptoms as a party in the body instead of a phenomenon to make us even *more* afraid.

Of course, fear isn't just about our physiological reaction. It's also about what the mind tells us about the dangers we face. That's exactly why reframing it in the mind is so important.

When I wrote my one-woman show a few years ago, it was an enormous undertaking, and I put a lot of time and effort into it, including hiring an experienced director. Finally, opening night arrived, and every seat in the audience was filled. As I stood backstage, ready to go on, terror set in. I had all of those same symptoms we've been talking about. Then the negative self-talk began. "Oh my goodness, you're so dumb, Erin. This is a terrible idea. What were you thinking? Are you an idiot? Why would you put yourself through this?"

My fear voice definitely has a tendency to exaggerate. "You *always* mess this up." "You'll *never* get that job." I think it's stuck in adolescence. Honestly, what a drama queen!

I had a similar experience when I was scheduled to speak before hundreds of people at an event. "You never should've said yes to this. You're not smart or wise enough. Everybody's going to think you're stupid," the voice told me.

Then I started to think about how afraid I was, and I got that double whammy of *fear of my fear.* "Oh my gosh, my fears are taking me over, and now I'll *never* be able to get through this speech!" Wow—brutal, isn't it?

I'm not going to pretend that I wasn't truly afraid in these instances. Clearly, I was. Because of that self-talk, I couldn't just label my dry mouth as "excitement" like Boss Bruce was able to do. Certainly, it's been helpful to reframe my body's reaction to fear, but I needed to remedy the self-talk too.

First, I began to notice my "go-to" dialogue with myself and what it meant. Whenever I was afraid, I immediately went into a self-shaming story about how I wasn't smart enough and how I make "bad" choices. Those were my "fear patterns."

These patterns would play out every time I presented to a large group of strangers or shared new work online. I went through a cycle of excitement, followed by a shame cycle right before it was "go time." I knew I wouldn't be able to eliminate my fears entirely, but maybe I could cultivate more courage by lessening the fear as much as possible.

So first, I decided to try watching my fears from a place of curiosity. As I observed the negative voice, I was able to place a toe—just a toe in the beginning, and maybe even just my baby toe—out of the ugliness of the negative self-talk. That little piece of me was able to step out of the emotion of the fear pattern and just watch myself as if I were watching a character in a movie. I took an almost clinical approach to the observation. "Oh, that's where you go when you're afraid—into that familiar belief that you aren't good enough and can't make sound decisions. *Interesting.*"

Over time, I have continued to pay close attention to the voices that pop up, particularly before I do something out of my comfort zone. As a result, I've been able to get more and more of myself out of the fear pattern, leaving less of me stuck there. Today, I can hear that negative self-talk without being so taken in by it.

Does this mean the fear and negativity have gone away? Has the voice shut up? No . . . and no. It's all still there. But with practice, I've gotten better at dealing with it and not believing my own fear story.

As long as we're evolving and trying new things, fear is going to be there. It's just part of the human experience, especially if you're exploring outside of your comfort zone.

I don't even believe in "fearlessness." Do you know anyone who's truly fearless? Everybody feels afraid sometimes, and most of us are frightened a lot.

So what does a courageous person have that you don't have? They keep pushing forward through the fear, and they refuse to believe the story their body and mind try to tell them. That's why the mantra for this chapter is:

It's my time
Today's the day
I will feel the fear
And I will do it anyway!

This mantra is a great tool to help you defuse the voice of fear so that you don't believe that negative story quite so much. You'll feel the butterflies and the racing heart, but you'll start to party with the fear. You'll learn to say, "Okay, fear, thanks very much for your input, but I really want to do this. I'm going to do it and see what happens. If it turns out well, I'll enjoy it and learn a lot. If it doesn't turn out well, I'll still learn a lot that I can apply to my next experience. Let's party!" And when you move while repeating that mantra, it won't feel like lip service. Your body will help you believe it!

But first, let's explore that fear story you've been telling yourself.

Journaling Exercise #10: Your Fear Story to Your Courage Story

Give yourself 15 to 20 minutes for this journaling exercise to explore your fear patterns and write a new "courage story."

1. Think about the last time you were afraid of trying something new. Close your eyes, and to the best of your ability, take yourself back to that moment of fear. It doesn't have to be a major event. It can be the fear of speaking up at a work meeting when you have a good idea you want to share. Noticing the small ways fear affects you can be very helpful. What did you feel in your body? Write down whatever you can remember.
2. Did you immediately label your body's sensations as fear? Using the work example, did you sit there with your heart racing and think, *Why am I so afraid even though I know these people well?* Imagine how the experience would have been different if you were able to reframe those sensations as excitement like Bruce Springsteen. Maybe you were actually excited to contribute your ideas to your team. Do you think reframing it might have helped you feel less afraid?
3. Try to remember your self-talk that last time you were afraid. What did you tell yourself could happen if you went through with the experience? How much did this inner voice derail you? Did you think you would be judged? Were you worried

about what might happen if you weren't successful? Did you feel the fear and do it anyway? Did it impair your ability to follow through, or did the fear get the best of you and stop you cold? Write down what you recall about your fear self-talk. (Note: This isn't an excuse to beat yourself up! It's just an opportunity to get to know yourself better so that you can change your behavior in the future.)

4. Think of another time you were afraid. Again, it can be a small, everyday event or something big. What can you recall about this experience? Do you remember your body's sensations? Do you remember your self-talk? Did you tell yourself you'd fail? Did your negative inner voice tell you that you weren't good enough? Did you feel you were in real danger? Write down what comes to mind.
5. If you can, recall a third time when you were afraid, and write down what you remember about it as well.
6. Look at what you wrote down for each fear experience. What themes do you see? Do you see themes like my "I'm stupid" and "I make bad choices" beliefs? These make up your personal "go-to" fear story—your greatest hits when fear wants to try to keep you safe from imagined dangers. Once you've identified them, you'll be conscious of what to expect. Your story will have less impact simply because you will know it's coming and be able to say, "Yeah, yeah, yada yada. Same old story."
7. One of the ways courageous people feel the fear and do it anyway is by telling themselves a *new* story. For example, instead of my story about how I'm stupid and make bad choices, I remind myself of all the times I've proven myself to be smart and of all the excellent choices I've made in the past. "Hey, Erin, you know you've had a lot of successes. You also know that successful people make a lot

of mistakes and have many failures before they achieve their goals. And you know what else? You'd be bored silly if you sat at home never taking any chances." Then I recall an instance in the past when I was successful after taking a risk. "Hey, Erin, remember that time you launched your videos, even though you didn't have any idea how to do it, and they took your business to a whole new level?" So let's rewrite your fear story into your *courage* story. What's a success story from your past that you can use to remind yourself of what's possible on the other side of your fear? Write it all down, and revisit it whenever your fear story threatens to take you in with its "fake news."

Before we move on, let's revisit our mantra:

It's my time
Today's the day
I will feel the fear
And I will do it anyway!

Five Important Points about Fear of Going After Your Dreams

1. Fear is a feeling. It isn't the truth.
2. Fear is related to a story you tell yourself that's almost always exaggerated and untrue.
3. As long as you're growing and trying new things, fear will always be there to some degree.
4. To gain more confidence, you have to feel the fear and do it anyway.
5. When you don't take action despite your fear, you usually feel worse because you keep yourself in a stagnant place with no growth, spontaneity, or challenges.

Courage before Confidence

On the opening night of my one-woman show, I was paralyzed with fear as I waited backstage. I'd rehearsed until I knew the material backward and forward, but this was the first time the show would be seen by anyone but the director. Suddenly, I couldn't find a single cell in my body that wanted to go out on that stage. Yikes.

But I had to get myself out there somehow. The audience was already in their seats waiting for me. If I sent them home without a show, I'd feel humiliated. Surely that would be worse than the fear of giving the performance.

Of course, I had no way of knowing if the show would go well. I could forget my lines, or everyone could hate it. I could walk away feeling like I should give up performing altogether.

Obviously, I had an important choice to make. I could surrender to the fear, or I could muster up the courage to step out and do the show I'd rehearsed. So I took a deep breath and stepped over all my uncertainty and fear. I faced the audience and did the show.

Since then, I've thought a lot about what got me out on that stage, especially when my clients make statements like, "I could reach my goal if I only had the confidence." "I just wish I believed in myself more. Then I could accomplish so much." But how can you have confidence that you'll succeed at something you've never tried before? I'd never done a one-woman show, so my confidence level was at a minimum. Instead, I had to let courage lead me *before* I had self-confidence. Oliver Wendell Holmes once said, "Courage is about doing what you're afraid to do. There can be no courage unless you're scared."

Confidence is great when you have it, but when you don't, it's courage that will propel you forward into inspired action. That's what got me out there on stage the night of my show. It's a classic chicken-and-egg question, and sometimes, the courage has to come *before* the confidence. As author Orison Swett Marden once said, "Most of our obstacles would melt away if, instead of cowering before them, we should make up our minds to walk boldly through them."

Once again, it's about feeling the fear and doing it anyway. I know that having the courage to take action is easier said than done, but that's what the exercises in this chapter and the movements with mantras are for. Then we're going to dive deep to find the courage you already have within. Moving your body while affirming your courage will get you past the paralysis that fear can cause.

Take Stock of Your Courage

"If I were truly brave, I'd take nonstop action and never let anybody's opinion stop me." That's what I've told myself on those occasions when I've let my fears get in my way. But isn't that a false notion of courage? That sounds like a superhero kind of bravery. I love Wonder Woman as much as the next girl, but I don't expect to become a superhero anytime soon.

Real bravery isn't about defeating a super villain. It's about getting out of bed when you're sick, feeding the kids, and delivering them to school. It's about showing up at the gym when what you really want to do is veg out on the couch with a box of doughnuts. It's about sending your résumé to your dream company when your inner voice says you don't have a chance at getting the job. It's about letting yourself feel your emotions when all you want to do is shut down.

Trust me—you're more courageous than you've ever given yourself credit for. If you weren't courageous, you wouldn't have learned how to walk. The first time you fell down, you would have given up. The first time you mispronounced a word, you would've stayed silent the rest of your life. You wouldn't have applied for a single job, gone on one date, or taken the slightest chance. And I'll bet you've taken more chances than you can possibly remember.

So if you think of yourself as a fearful person, think again. You've been way too hard on yourself.

Maybe you're courageous because you went to the doctor even though you were afraid it would hurt. Maybe you're courageous because you got out of bed on a day you were depressed. Maybe you're brave because you started a conversation with a stranger at a business function.

We think of courage as some big, daring gesture, but we're all brave every day in a number of ways. Courage is simply not giving up in the face of your own fear. Not giving in despite your self-doubt.

Every time you're brave—in whatever unique way is brave for you—you have the opportunity to generate more courage. You can build on what you already have and apply that energy to actions where the fear threatens to overtake your nerve. But first, you have to acknowledge the courageous version of you because that, my friend, is the truth of who you are.

So I'm hereby granting you a cape. In your own little world, you *are* a human version of Wonder Woman or Superman—just through every act of courage you make each day. Yes, even if you still cower in the corner at times. I challenge you to love yourself for both your cowardly moments and your courageous moments. Are you up to that challenge?

Here's a simple little example from my own life. Living in New York City, I see celebrities pretty regularly. In the past, I couldn't get up the courage to say, "Thank you for your wonderful work. I simply loved you in '___________.'" Instead, I walked away feeling like a coward because I couldn't muster up those few words. And as silly as it sounds, I'd beat myself up for it the rest of the day.

Then I began to love my cowardly self and forgive that part of me for not being able to step out of her comfort zone. Rather than beat myself up, I sent love to this sweet part of myself who was so worried about sounding stupid. I gave her a bit of a break and reminded myself that there would always be another chance.

And guess what? Once I began to treat myself with more kindness and compassion, my behavior shifted. Now when I see an actor, politician, or artist I admire, I have absolutely no problem at all telling them how much I appreciate them. I now see myself as someone who is equally as wonderful as they are, so there's no reason to be intimidated. And of course, this ability to have compassion for myself has allowed me to take more risks in all areas of my life. Once I no longer expected myself to be perfect, I was more willing to try things I might otherwise be afraid of. This, my friend, is the power of doing the work that is laid out in this book.

So while you learn to love yourself for your cowardly moments, let's acknowledge the moments when you show courage, even if it's in small ways.

Journaling Exercise #11: Increase the Size of Your Courage

In *The Wizard of Oz,* the Tin Man wanted a heart and the Cowardly Lion wanted courage. But the truth is that courage lives in the heart. When people in sports talk about an athlete with "heart," they mean courage. So let's increase the size of your courage by recognizing where you already have heart.

1. Complete this sentence as many times as you wish, but try to complete it at least five times. I suggest writing it down so that you can refer to it the next time you get down on yourself for feeling afraid:

   Every day, I'm afraid of ______________________

   ______________________, and every day, I show

   courage by ______________________.

   Every day, I'm afraid of ______________________

   ______________________, and every day, I show

   courage by ______________________.

Every day, I'm afraid of ______________________

______________________, and every day, I show

courage by ______________________.

Every day, I'm afraid of ______________________

______________________, and every day, I show

courage by ______________________.

Every day, I'm afraid of ______________________

______________________, and every day, I show

courage by ______________________.

2. During the coming week, notice your courageous actions, no matter how small you deem them to be. If you can, make note of them in a notebook or on your device.
3. At the end of the week, reward yourself for your courage with a special gift. Just make sure it's loving and within your budget. Maybe you'll buy yourself some flowers, treat yourself to a movie, or get a massage. What about a relaxing soak with your favorite scented oil or bubble bath? Maybe all you want is to make time for a visit to your favorite place. Write in your calendar when you'll collect your reward.
4. Make a pact with yourself that you'll notice more of your courageous actions from now on and give yourself the credit you're due. Don your cape!

The Courage to Speak Up for Yourself

When I arrived in Los Angeles for the second season of *Altar'd*, I was 18 weeks pregnant. Production knew that my growing belly would be a part of the show, and they were excited to work it into the storyline.

Just a few weeks before, I'd been diagnosed with a blood clot near my cervix that caused severe bleeding. It was a scary time, and the doctor had asked me to take it easy. So it was especially important to me to have a place to stay in LA that was comfortable and allowed for minimal walking.

The production team booked me in an apartment that looked like exactly what I needed. I'd call it home for almost three months. But when I woke up the morning after my first night there, I noticed that one of my tote bags had a hole in it, and the hole was surrounded by bite marks. *Oh no!* I thought, *my apartment has a rat*!

I immediately called my husband, who was planning to join me in a few weeks. "What? A rat? That's unacceptable!" he said. "Erin, you're moving out of there. Tell production to find you a new place right away."

I knew he was right. There was no reason anybody, let alone a pregnant woman, should have to live with a rat. But I was still afraid to call the production team. The people pleaser in me thought they'd label me a "diva." That little voice inside me said, "They won't like you anymore."

But I mustered up my courage and called them. "Would you look into getting an exterminator here?" I asked. Maybe, I thought, I could avoid rocking the boat *too much* if I settled for this compromise.

Production called the landlord, but the landlord was not at all helpful. Even after production called the exterminator, I realized that I still felt extremely uncomfortable about staying there. How could I know for sure that the rats were gone and that the poison wasn't toxic to me and my baby? But since I hadn't asked for what I really wanted, production responded with "Can you make it work?"

Unfortunately, by compromising and trying hard not to inconvenience anyone, I'd brought my wishy-washy self to the table. No one was going to go out of their way to help me unless I put my foot down. I needed to get the boat rockin'.

So instead of saying, "Sure, I can make it work," I said, "The landlord is not being helpful. I'm not comfortable there, knowing there could be more rats, so I need a new apartment. It's production's responsibility to move me." I simply stated what I wanted without any emotion. I didn't apologize, and I refused to worry about anyone else's inconvenience. Once I was clear with them, I got what I wanted quickly and was moved to a new apartment that provided what I needed—minimal walking and *no rats*!

The truth is that moving toward our dreams requires that we speak up for ourselves and ask for what we want. While men struggle with it as well, it seems even harder for many women. I have a friend who hired two copywriters, one male and one female. He offered them both the same exact salary. The man asked for more money and got it, while the woman never asked for more. She accepted the given amount that was presented to her. This story blew me away. How often do we sabotage ourselves simply because we don't realize what we're worth?

Simply put, courage is a lot about being willing to rock the boat because we know we deserve better.

My personal role model/action figure in this area is Congresswoman Maxine Waters. Not long before I wrote this, she questioned Secretary of the Treasury Steven Mnuchin in a formal hearing. He continuously refused to answer her directly. Each time he tried to skate her question and wasted the time she was allotted, she repeated, "Reclaiming my time. Reclaiming my time. Reclaiming my time." It became a mantra of its own for many of us! If you haven't seen the video of this, please search for it and watch it. You will be inspired!

Maxine showed such courage in those moments, and one of the key ways she did that was by *letting go of her concern about being liked*. She was much more concerned about getting the outcome she wanted. And that is where I want you to begin to place your attention. Imagine what it would feel like to be more focused on getting what you want rather than whether or not someone likes you. I'm not saying you have license to walk all over someone else, but people pleasing prevents us from progress more often than we realize.

I'm sure Maxine didn't come out of the womb with the kind of courage she has now. She had to cultivate it and take those baby steps toward her current level of courage. When you focus your attention on the outcome you want and dial down the emotion, you, too, can begin to cultivate more and more courage.

Remember our mantra:

It's my time
Today's the day
I will feel the fear
And I will do it anyway!

Journaling Exercise #12: Reclaim Your Time

Allot about 15 minutes for this exercise. You'll explore your fears with regard to a specific situation and begin to move forward anyway.

- Think of a time when you were spurred into action. Maybe it was an experience of speaking up for yourself. Write down what you remember feeling prior to taking action.
- Reread your answer to #1. Were you afraid before you took action? If so, what helped you move forward despite your fear? What gave you the courage to speak up?
- Think of a current situation in which fear is stopping you in your tracks—a place where you feel stuck. Maybe you want to apply for your dream job, but you've been too scared to do it. Reread your answer to #2. Is there anything in your past

experience of taking action in spite of your fear that might help you strengthen your courage now?

- Like you did in Chapter 5, write down 1 to 5 baby steps you can take to muster up your courage. *Example: I've been wanting to tell my boss that I need more time to finish the monthly reports. Right now it's virtually impossible to get them done on schedule. Here are my baby steps:*

    1. *Write down the problem as I see it.*
    2. *Write down the solution that I propose.*
    3. *Memorize what I've written, and practice saying it in front of the mirror to gather my courage before asking to speak to my boss.*
    4. *Get my colleague Laura to listen to my pitch to the boss and give me feedback.*
    5. *Visualize my boss agreeing with me.*

- Make a pact with yourself to take these baby steps within the next two weeks. If you don't think you'll stick to the pact, write a contract with yourself and promise yourself a reward for maintaining your pact for the two weeks—perhaps a massage or even just an extra hour of sleep. If your baby steps still don't quite move you to the action you want to take, write down more steps when you finish with your first baby steps. Let's get you to that place of reclaiming your time!

Choose Courage over Comfort

Your comfort zone is a cozy, safe place that feels like a warm blanket. There's a lot to be said for that, and there are times when you absolutely need to snuggle in the arms of that comfort zone. But there's a balance to be found between forgiving your cowardly self and pushing yourself out of your comfort zone. If you stay in that cozy little zone all the time, your life will become a terrible bore, and all that potential you were born with? It's just squandered, left unused like expensive sheets that are saved for company that never comes. Those sheets sit in their package until they wear out from age but never from use. I don't know about you, but that makes me feel sad.

As author Debbie Ford said, "Our fear of change, our fear of stepping into new realities, is so deep that we desperately cling to the world we know. We often mistake familiarity for safety. The perceived comfort we derive from what's familiar keeps us living in the illusion of our story."

Life requires that we step out of our comfort zone at least some of the time. If the very idea makes you shake in your shoes, try this: watch a movie in which the main character is heroic in some way. A classic go-to in this category is *Rudy*. It's the true story of a boy who dreams of playing football with Notre Dame. His story is more about his unwavering courage than about his success. He's the epitome of an athlete with heart. When you watch *Rudy* or your own go-to story about someone who triumphs over adversity, put yourself into the movie. See yourself as the heroic character. Feel it. Be it. This is a way you can practice stepping out of your comfort zone and seeing yourself as the courageous person you already are and can be.

MANTRA IN MOTION #5

When fear stops you, the best way I've found to move through it is to . . . well, *move!* And when you add a courage mantra to that, you have a recipe for leaving fear in the dust! Let's not waste another minute. Today's the day for the courageous you to step up.

Your Courage Mantra

It's my time
Today's the day
I will feel the fear
And I will do it anyway!

Move 1: Single Leg Lunge

Line 1: *It's my time*
What if you no longer waited on the sidelines of your life? What if you decided that this is your time? You don't have to wait for perfection or until you have all the answers, and you certainly don't have to wait until someone gives you permission. It's your time. Let's go!

"It's my time"

1. Start with your feet together and your hands in prayer pose at your heart. Stand strong in this pose.
2. Step your right leg back into a lunge, bending both knees. Be sure to track your left knee directly over your left ankle. Bring your hands down to a *V* position. As you step back, say, "It's my . . ."
3. Step your feet back together and say, ". . . time." You want to feel the energy of stepping the feet together on return. *This is one rep.*
4. You will repeat the same move on the other side. Alternate sides with each lunge, repeating this 8 times on each side for a total of 16 reps.

Move 2: Plié Touch Down

Line 2: *Today's the day*
Imagine for a moment that the next 30 seconds are the most important 30 seconds of your whole day. How would you treat those 30 seconds? How would you treat yourself in that time? Now imagine that today is the most important day of your life. I invite you to approach these movements as if there truly were no day but today!

"Today's the day"

1. Stand with your feet in a wide plié squat. With your legs bent, bend your upper body down and touch the floor with both hands.
2. As you reach to the floor, say, "Today's the . . ."
3. As you come back up, extend your arms out in front of you with your hands in a triangle as you say, ". . . day."
4. Repeat this, touching down to the floor and pressing up and out through your arms. You'll feel a stretch in your legs. Perform 16 reps of this movement and mantra.

Move 1: Single Leg Lunge

Line 3: *I will feel the fear*
We have discussed fear several times throughout this chapter. Hopefully by now you understand that it's absolutely normal to feel afraid. During this move and mantra, I invite you to party with your fear! Transform it into something more powerful like excitement!

"I will feel the fear"

1. Start with your feet together and your hands in prayer pose at your heart. Stand strong in this pose.
2. Step your right leg back into a lunge, bending both knees. Be sure to track your left knee directly over your left ankle. Bring your hands down to a *V* position. As you step back, say, "I will feel the . . ."
3. Step your feet back together and say, ". . . fear." As you step up, feel yourself stepping into whatever fear you might have. You can do it. *This is one rep.*
4. You will repeat the same move on the other side. Alternate sides with each lunge, repeating this 8 times on each side for a total of 16 reps.

Move 2: Plié Touch Down

Line 4: *And I will do it anyway*
This is your "no excuse" moment. Fear and worry won't stop you today. This is your time to call up those few moments of insane courage and do what you've set out to do, no matter what.

"And I will do it anyway"

1. Stand with your feet in a wide plié squat. With your legs bent, bend your upper body down, and touch the floor with both hands.
2. As you reach to the floor, say, "And I will do it . . ."
3. As you come back up, extend your arms out in front of you with your hands in a triangle as you say, ". . . anyway."
4. Repeat this, touching down to the floor and pressing up and out through your arms. You'll feel a stretch in your legs. Perform 16 reps of this movement and mantra.

Putting It All Together

Now you're going to put the whole cycle together for 10 cycles. Alternate between Move 1 and Move 2. Hopefully, you're getting comfortable with the moves, and the mantras are starting to stick.

Do one move with one line at a time so it will flow like this:

Move 1: Single Leg Lunge
Mantra: *It's my time*
(Do just one lunge on your right side. Then step out to your second position plié to perform the next move and mantra.)

Move 2: Plié Touch Down
Mantra: *Today's the day*
(After you perform this move and mantra, take a pause, and bring your feet back together in order to do the next move on your left *side.)*

Move 1: Single Leg Lunge
Mantra: *I will feel the fear*
(Do the lunge on your left leg only before stepping back out into the plié squat position.)

Move 2: Plié Touch Down
Mantra: *And I will do it anyway*
(After you perform this move and mantra, you will have completed one cycle. Bring your feet back together to start again.) You will repeat this whole cycle 10 times.

GATHER YOUR SUPPORT SYSTEM

One of my Shrink Session clients was so excited to enroll in a supervised behavioral weight-loss program, only to find that it wasn't at all what she expected. When she shared with her group that Shrink Session had helped her move out of the obese range and lose 40 pounds, her group members snickered and scowled. There wasn't a single "Congratulations!" No one gave her a high five. The group that was designed to support her was unable to walk with her through the very transformation they all claimed they were headed toward.

It was painful. Devastating, in fact.

The couples on *Altar'd* have had similar experiences, but in their cases, it's often a lack of support from their significant other. Some have struggled with weight all their lives, while others gained weight after they became a couple.

As they're separated from each other for 90 days, the time apart allows them to create new habits, learn new tools, and develop self-confidence on their own. It also prevents them from enabling each other to stick to their old habits.

What we've found is that a lot of them have served as bad influences on their partners. One of them will say, "We should go to the gym and get in some exercise."

The other will then say something like, "No, let's watch TV instead." The next thing they know, they're both on the couch, relinquishing their exercise commitment, maybe even sharing some ice cream or a box of cookies.

Since it might feel better in the moment to sit on the couch than sweat at the gym, the couples feel as though they're giving each other support. But that "support" is a wolf in a sheep suit.

Some of the couples have been unable to continue to make their relationships work after coming back together following their 90 days apart. Maybe one of them managed to commit to changing, but the other one didn't. Some of those who have worked hard to feel healthier and look better haven't been willing to be with someone who won't support them in their new way of life.

I'd be lying if I said it hasn't been painful to watch couples split up over this, but it's also been inspiring. At least two of the women have gone back to school to get the education they've always wanted. Making those changes in their lifestyle gave them the courage to follow their dreams, even if it meant letting another dream go. I don't know if I've ever been prouder of people I've worked with! They've motivated me to make more of a commitment to my own dreams, even if it means making a sacrifice.

And that's exactly what my client in the behavioral weight-loss program had to do. She had to sacrifice being in the group. That was far from fun for her, but if they weren't going to support her new life, what else could she do? She wasn't willing to gain back the weight just so they'd feel comfortable. She had to come to terms with the fact that the group would be a part of her past. She allowed the Shrink Session online community to support her going forward, where she connected with people who applauded and encouraged her transformation.

How many of us have been in this position? How often are we in relationships that we expect will be supportive, only to find out that the opposite is true? We want to make a life change, try something new, or just take a risk. Yet people in our lives try to talk us out of it, tell us we're making a mistake, or maybe even make fun of us and put us down. "Oh, you'll never be able to get that job." "You've always had your head in the clouds. I can't believe you think you're so high and mighty that you can apply to that school." "You want to go rock climbing? You'll end up killing yourself!" "Who are you to write a book?"

These comments are particularly painful when they come from the people closest to us—our significant other, parents, siblings, or best friends. But think of all the world-changing accomplishments that would never have happened if people throughout history had listened to the naysayers in their lives. Then imagine all the accomplishments we *have* missed out on because of the people who *did* listen to the naysayers in their lives. It's a shame for sure.

Big life changes are scary, and distancing ourselves from people who refuse to support us can make it more frightening. But often, that's exactly what we're called to do if we want to follow our hearts, reach our full potential, and create the sweet life we deserve.

Why do we attract people who won't offer us the support we want and need? Often, they're a reflection of our own fears and insecurities. And, of course, that's why their voices are hard to ignore. If someone tells you that you can't do something when you're already afraid you can't, they only reinforce your fear. When it's a parent or sibling reiterating the same negativity you've heard all your life—negativity that has become an integral part of your own internal put-downs and discouragement—it takes a lot of courage to say, "No! I'm not going to listen to you or my fear. Even if I fail, I'm going to try because I'll have already failed if I don't try at all. No matter what, I'll learn a lot, and maybe—just maybe—I'll succeed and enter a new phase of my life."

This step is all about support—the support you already have and the support you can gather that will help you manifest your dreams. Ready for your mantra?

I release my doubts
It's all working out
Support is all around
I am breaking new ground!

How Much Will You Tolerate?

My friend Pam told me a story about how she had taken all sorts of abuse from a female friend for several years. The woman put Pam down, tried to convince her she wouldn't succeed, and basically treated her like a punching bag. For a long time, Pam tolerated it because her own self-esteem wasn't strong enough to say, "This isn't right!" Her friend echoed Pam's own inner self-talk.

Then the friend moved away, and Pam started attending self-development workshops and seeing a therapist. She quickly learned that she only allowed her friend to hurt her because of low self-worth. So she began working on changing her self-talk, increasing her self-support, and no longer talking to herself in an abusive way. When she had occasion to see her friend again, the abuse started just like before. This time, however, Pam wasn't willing to tolerate it. She let her "friend" know that it wasn't the kind of relationship she wanted, and she wouldn't allow herself to be treated that way anymore. She didn't hear from the friend again, but she knew she was better off and hasn't regretted it for a moment.

I had a similar experience with a close girlfriend who would become abusive whenever we argued. She had a more dominant personality, so I always thought I was at fault. *She must be right, and I must've done something wrong,* I thought. This went on for a long time until I experienced a turning point from doing the same kind of work I've laid out in the book. I began to treat myself with more kindness and respect. Through the journaling work, meditation, and repetition of the mantras and movement, I learned that we only allow people to treat us as well as we're willing to treat ourselves.

After one particular argument with my friend, I finally said, "I don't treat myself like that anymore, so you don't get to talk to me that way either."

It can be painful to walk away from friends, but it's usually even harder to walk away from family members. If we grow up with people who frequently discourage us, it's more comfortable to stay where we are than to challenge that status quo. Still, we have to ask ourselves: How much are we willing to tolerate? It doesn't mean that we have to disown our parents, grandparents, or siblings. But we may have to distance ourselves to some degree in order to be shielded from the hurtful onslaught. The only alternative is to become strong enough within ourselves that the hurtful, discouraging comments bounce off without penetrating. The more self-love, self-respect, and self-support we generate from within, the more our own feelings about ourselves become like a bullet-proof vest.

Journaling Exercise #13: What's Your Support Quotient?

Give yourself 15 to 20 minutes for this journaling exercise. Ask yourself the following questions, and write down your answers in a journal or on a device.

- Are you currently in any relationships or involved in any groups that are not supportive of you? If so, in what ways are they not supportive, either physically or emotionally? What have you tolerated up to this point?

  Example: My writers' group allows participants to give snarky criticism that isn't productive or helpful. I've tolerated it, even though it's been emotionally hurtful.

- How does it feel to lack the support from these people and/or groups, and how do you behave as a result of this lack of support?

  Example: It feels lousy to receive no support from the writers' group. Often, it feels like they just criticize one another in order to build themselves up. As a result, I cower in the group and rarely say anything. I've also considered giving up writing entirely.

- If you received the support you need, what would it look like? Can you envision that kind of support?

  Example: I don't mind constructive criticism at all. In fact, I welcome it. I'd love it if people could find something nice to say about my work and then move on to suggestions that I could really use. That's what I hoped the group would be like.

- How would it feel if you had this support, and how would you behave differently if you had it?

  Example: If I had that kind of support, I'd participate much more in the group. I wouldn't feel like everything I said was going to be scrutinized and put down. I'm also sure I'd become a better writer with constructive criticism and some praise mixed in.

- What people or groups *are* supportive of you? In what ways do they support you?

  Example: I have a professional writer friend who loves my writing and is the main reason I haven't given it up. She's always willing to read my work and offer ways to make it better, as well as give me business advice.

- Where in your life do you need more support? For example, could you use more emotional support from friends or family members? Would it be helpful to have assistance in taking care of your kids or the house? Would you appreciate encouragement from others for a new project?

  Example: I feel like my writing is treated like a whim or a silly hobby. So I could use both emotional and physical support from my partner. I would love to have set days to go to my favorite spot to write while my partner takes the kids. I also want to come home from my writing sessions and find the house in order so that I don't have more work to do. I'd like to know that my partner can manage both the kids and the home while I write.

- Who can you ask for the support you need? If you can't think of anyone, make a commitment to continue to look for people or groups who could help you. My Shrink Session program has a wonderfully supportive Facebook community filled with people all over the world who lift one another up on a daily basis. I also have a Facebook and Instagram page if you search for "Erin Stutland." I love to give people support through all of these pages. I hope you will seek me out so that I can become part of your support system!

Example: I'm going to visit Erin's Facebook page and look for a different writing group. I'm also going to ask my partner for help around the house so that I can have dedicated time for my writing.

- Where in your life do you already receive support, and who provides that support? Think about all areas in your life—home, neighborhood, community, work, family relationships, friendships, health, recreation, etc. What support do you have in each of these areas? For example, in the community, you have a postal worker, sanitation workers, friendships, or maybe even someone to cut your grass. You don't have to write them all down unless you want to, but at least take a moment to appreciate the people and systems that are there for you, and recognize that you already have more support than you realized! Doesn't that feel good?
- Right now, affirm to yourself that you'll allow yourself to receive more. I promise you that you deserve it!

Why Is It So Hard to Ask For and Accept Support?

Have you ever automatically said no when someone offered you support? Maybe they asked to help you carry a bag or drive you to the airport, but you said, "No, I'm fine." Some of us refuse this help even though we're desperate for it. We can't accept—let alone ask for—support because underneath it all, we believe we don't deserve it. Or we're afraid people will think we're a bother. There are those nasty limiting beliefs again!

Sometimes we're concerned about owing others. We feel we have to reciprocate if we accept help. There are no rules here, but would you truly mind reciprocating? You don't have to give back right away. If you feel you'll have nothing to offer the other person, say so with regret. Chances are, they'll be happy for the opportunity to give without hope of reciprocation. If you don't know when you'll be able to reciprocate, say that too. "I don't know when I can do the same for you, but I hope to get that opportunity someday. I appreciate your help so much."

Some of us are afraid to ask because we might be turned down. That's a real possibility, of course, but we have to remind ourselves that being turned down has nothing to do with our self-worth. It may not even have anything to do with how the other person feels about us. They may simply not be able to help in this instance for some reason.

Others of us believe that vulnerability or allowing ourselves to be seen as less than 100 percent capable will put us at some risk. That's a false belief based on perfectionism. Everyone needs help sometimes. There's no shame in it.

We make all sorts of excuses for not asking for the help we need. "If my house weren't such a mess, I could hire a cleaning person." "If I made more money in my business, I could hire the right person." We don't think that it's wise to invest in the right person to help us make more money!

What about you—are you willing to ask for support? Then, when you do, are you willing to receive it gracefully? Think of how wonderful it feels to help others. Whenever you refuse to accept assistance, you deny the other person that warm, fuzzy feeling. Make a pact with yourself to (1) accept support when it's offered unless there's a truly good reason to turn it down, and (2) ask for support more often.

If asking for support is difficult for you, review your answer to the seventh bullet point in the previous exercise. Who on your list will be the easiest person to ask for help? Write down what you'll say to him/her, and set a date when you'll ask.

I find the best way to request anything is to put it in a "thank-you sandwich." This means that your first piece of "bread" involves acknowledging the other person for something they've done for you. The "meat" of the sandwich is your request, and the second piece of "bread" is another compliment, acknowledgment, or expression of gratitude.

Let's use our example of requesting more support from our partner. First piece of bread: "Thank you for the help around the house this weekend. I really appreciate it, and I know the kids love spending time with you."

Meat of the sandwich: "As you know, I'd love to spend more time writing. I'm excited about my current project and want to treat it seriously. In order to do this, I need your support. Could we adjust our schedules so that I have three hours of uninterrupted writing time two days a week while you watch the kids?"

Second piece of bread: "I love the way you step up and parent our children. I want us both to be the best versions of ourselves and hope we can make this happen together."

Practice your request, and psych yourself up for it. Remind yourself several times a day that you deserve this support and have every right to ask for it. Think of all the times someone asked you for support, and you were thrilled to be of service. Also, affirm to yourself that if this person says no, you won't take it personally. You'll take a deep breath before negotiating further with this person, or you'll move on to the next person on your list. If you do find yourself taking it personally, guess what? It's an opportunity to practice smart self-talk, reminding that hurt child inside you that the other person's inability to help has nothing to do with your worth!

On that note, let's reiterate our mantra:

I release my doubts
It's all working out
Support is all around
I am breaking new ground!

Life Supports You More Than You Realize

It's easy to feel like a victim, telling ourselves that we don't have the support we need. We can feel like life is working against us at every turn, refusing to provide sufficient emotional and physical nourishment. But I contend that life supports you much more than you've probably ever acknowledged.

I assume as you read this, you're sitting on a chair or couch. Do you have to do anything to make that chair or couch support you? It's just there for you, isn't it? If you're indoors, the roof over your head is supporting you, too, keeping you safe and shielding you from the elements. Outside, the sun gives you light, the clouds give you rain, the trees give you shade, the birds give you song, and the earth gives you ground to walk on.

Your heart is beating on its own, supporting your life without any effort from you. Your lungs are breathing in and out, supporting you with the oxygen you need to live. The air is just there for you to take in. When you were a child, you didn't make yourself grow into an adult. You simply grew!

Of course, the support that life provides doesn't mean we're spared life's challenges or tragedies. It's easy to believe in that support when all is well, but what about when the you-know-what hits the fan? That's when it's even more important to respond with as much faith as we can muster.

Even with all the work of creating mindfulness in my life and in my interactions with others, I'm far from perfect at staying in faith when life doesn't go as planned. But I believe it's my responsibility to always look for the many ways that Life supports me. As an example, after I turned my Shrink Session teacher-training curriculum into an apprenticeship program, one of my trainees landed her dream job . . . elsewhere. She'd be performing in a show that would take her out of New York for six months. While teaching Shrink Session was an exciting new chapter for her, performing was still her heart and soul. She was afraid to tell me because she knew I was counting on her to start teaching, but she couldn't turn down that job.

I have to be candid with you: my first reaction wasn't "Wow! I'm so excited for you!" Under a variety of different circumstances, that would have been my normal response. But because her leaving would directly affect what I'd envisioned for the next six months, let's just say that this loving response wasn't available to me in that moment. Instead, my first internal reaction was, "Are you kidding me? I've just spent a month training you, and now I've wasted time and energy on you!"

But I don't yell when I'm upset. Instead, I get quiet, which can come off as passive-aggressive while I struggle to hide and push down my feelings. I was well aware that quiet aggression wasn't a good look on me, so I first took what I call a "MATO," which stands for "Mini Adult Time Out." This simply involved taking some time to breathe and keep my mouth shut until I could better manage my anger using some of my favorite mantras. I told myself, "If I believe that life supports me everywhere I go, then surely this situation is in my best interest, as well as hers."

Once I had a handle on my feelings, I told my apprentice the truth. "Look, this is hard to hear. If you're not getting warm, fuzzy feelings from me, it's just because I have a lot of feelings about this. I want to support you, but at the same time, my ego is doing a little fear dance. I do know that ultimately, this will work out for the best for both of us." Then I listened to her internal conflicts about the situation. As I heard her feelings, my own fears began to soften. I let her know that the door was always open for her to return, and we hugged.

It took me some time to work through all my disappointment, but I immediately shifted my focus to working on a solution to the problem. There were other trainees who needed a little more work but had great promise. I could focus on getting them ready sooner than I thought. It was a much more powerful position because I was looking forward, where change was possible, rather than in the past, where change was futile.

Finally, I reminded myself that in every moment, we're either giving love or we're taking it away. We're either living in faith or in fear. I could stay angry and disappointed, or I could take action to fix the problem.

So as difficult as it can be when setbacks occur, we're called upon to continue to believe in the support that is always ours. There just may be a greater wisdom at work than we can see.

Sometimes we're being prepared for something better than we can imagine. Other times, we don't get what we want right away because we need to build certain skills and strengths on the way, or the timing isn't right yet. Perhaps we have to take certain steps that will help us clarify what we *truly* want.

Look, I know all too well that it's easy to lose heart and even feel like life wants us to suffer, but I contend that nothing could be further from the truth. Despite the setbacks and hurts you experience, life itself, which created you, is in constant support of you and your growth. Let's tune in to this energetic support that life continuously offers you.

Meditation #3: Support from Life Itself

If you can remember this meditation, read through it, and then close your eyes to walk yourself through the steps. Or you can record yourself reading it and play it back while you meditate. Better yet, go to my website and listen to the audio at www.erinstutland.com/gifts. It should take no more than 5 to 10 minutes.

1. For this meditation, please lie down on the floor. Begin by closing your eyes and slowly relaxing each part of your body from your feet all the way up to the top of your head. Simply say, "I relax my feet, I relax my legs," and so forth. If there's a chance you'll fall asleep, don't spend too much time relaxing your body.
2. As you lie on the floor, feel its support underneath you. It's supporting your head, your shoulders, your torso, your arms and hands, your hips, your legs, and your feet. Connect with the parts of your body that are supporting you in this moment—your beating heart, your breathing lungs, your organs that are continuing to function without your conscious involvement, your ears, your eyelids that have closed so that you can focus within, your mouth that allows you to taste and swallow.
3. Breathe deeply, and feel how much life and the world around you support you every moment of every day. Drink it in, and allow yourself to feel grateful.

4. Take a moment to thank all the support structures that require so little of you. Thank the building you're in, and thank your body for its ongoing support. Appreciate all of it as much as you can, and affirm that you'll no longer take this immense support for granted.
5. When you're ready, open your eyes, and get up off the floor.

Journaling Exercise #14: Your Own Personal "Life Support"

This exercise is in two parts and should take 10 to 15 minutes. The first part is an ongoing writing exercise that was created by my coach, Julie-Anne Lee Kinney. She has generously allowed me to include it here. The second is another writing exercise to help you reach a goal using your own inner support.

Part 1: The Evidence Journal

At the end of each day or throughout the day, take note of the many small and large ways in which life supports you. As you notice more and more of the support you already receive, you'll feel less like a victim, and you'll feel regular gratitude.

Examples of what you might write down:

1. *My goal is to get out of financial debt, and when I went to Starbucks this morning, I found out I was eligible for a free coffee.*
2. *In my car on the way to work, my favorite song came on the radio, and it immediately changed my mood for the better.*
3. *A stranger smiled at me and filled my heart.*
4. *I woke up from a particularly deep night's sleep, leaving me rested and ready for the day ahead.*

5. *I had dinner out, and there was enough food left over for lunch the next day.*
6. *I saw an opportunity to open the door for an elderly person, and it made me feel good to help someone.*
7. *I fed the birds in the park, and it lifted my spirits to give these tiny beings the sustenance they need to survive.*

Part 2: Work toward a Goal

In this journaling exercise, you'll work toward creating something you want.

1. Choose a goal or object you want to create for yourself. For example, you might want to achieve stronger self-confidence, or you might want to manifest a trip to Europe or a new car.
2. Start by thinking about what resources you already have to manifest this. If you want to achieve stronger self-confidence, you could note the confidence you've already generated within, supportive friends who are willing to remind you of your good qualities, books that you can read, podcasts you can listen to, workshops that you can attend, and coaches you can work with. If you're working toward creating a trip to Europe or a new car, what support/resources do you have? Perhaps you have some income that you can save every week or month toward your goal. Maybe you know someone who can tell you about deals that would get you a better price. If you investigate, you might already have credit card or membership points you can use toward a plane ticket or hotel stay. Write down everything you can think of that you already have to support you in your goal. Continue to add to this list as new resources come to mind.

3. If there is something on this list that feels like an action you can take, I invite you to add it to your action list that you started in Chapter 5. This way, you're constantly noticing the support that's available to you and acting on it.
4. And as you work toward your goal, remember your mantra:

I release my doubts
It's all working out
Support is all around
I am breaking new ground!

Your Internal Support Structure

After working with a teacher and being part of her community for some time, I got a strong feeling that it was time to go out on my own to develop my own coaching and teaching method. Yet I'd relied on that community for a long time. They were an important part of my life, so preparing for the break with them turned me into an emotional wreck. I feared they'd be angry with me and I'd lose every single one of them.

In this case, unfortunately, my fears came true. Many people in the community were upset with my choice to leave, and they didn't want me in their lives anymore. Ouch. It was painful to know that I was disappointing them. Losing my tribe felt awful.

At first, I tolerated their objections because a part of me felt their opinions were more valid than my own. I had the old "They must be right because what do I know?" syndrome.

Was I making the right choice? Had I been mistaken about what my heart was calling me to do?

When I answered that question sincerely, I had to say, "I wasn't mistaken at all! I've made the right choice for me."

My next question was, "If they can't support this decision, can I support myself?" I could allow these other voices to be stronger than my own, or I could allow *my* voice to be the strongest. In this circumstance, I had to be the one who stood up for myself, believing in my dreams and decisions.

Then something extraordinary happened. When I committed to my own inner support structure, that commitment was reflected back to me, as I attracted more and more people who offered me the outer support I wanted and needed. It wasn't long before I started new classes, attracted more students who loved my work, and began to build a team of employees who were excited to help me bring my vision to life.

As hard as it is to ask others to support us and allow them to help us, it's even harder for most of us to give ourselves support from within—especially when the people we wanted to support us said no. Even if we finally refuse to accept verbal abuse from others, we still often verbally abuse ourselves on the inside. "You decided to leave your group, and see what happened, Erin? You lost everybody. Now what are you going to do? Good job!" The negative self-talk can be relentless. We would never dream of saying to someone else what we say to ourselves. If we don't accept it from others, why do we accept it from ourselves? It's the opposite of self-support.

In those moments when we don't have support from others, it's up to us to step up and give ourselves what we need. It takes self-awareness, and it takes commitment. It comes down to what you'll tolerate—in this case, not from others but from yourself. Will you continue to tolerate the onslaught of abuse in your own mind?

Just like we become accustomed to tolerating negative comments from others, we become accustomed to our own negative self-talk. It's comfortable because it's what we know. It's a bad habit, and changing habits requires work.

Another issue that we need to be aware of is false self-support. Just like some of the couples on *Altar'd* enabled each other to continue eating, we do the same for ourselves. It feels like self-support when we eat something unhealthy because it's so satisfying in the moment. But we're only supporting one part of us—the part that doesn't want to feel our emotions. This is the part that wants to stuff our unpleasant feelings down with the comfort of a piece of cake. But we *aren't* supporting the part of us that's having the feelings or the part that wants to feel healthy. Again, we tolerate feeling worse about ourselves for a longer period of time in order to have those brief moments of instant gratification. And it's all because we don't figure out what we *truly* need in those moments.

When we give ourselves real self-support, we ask ourselves what we really need when we have the urge to eat an unhealthy food or procrastinate or go on a shopping binge or allow our mean boyfriend back into our lives. When I ask myself this question, the answer might be that I need to sit down and hold myself, allowing tears to come (even if I don't know why or would rather not). Maybe I need to scream into a pillow. Maybe I need true sweetness in my life, such as a hug or kind words from my partner or a friend. I can ask myself, "What will procrastinating or binge shopping or staying with my mean boyfriend give to me that I could give to myself right now? Is there someone else I can ask to support me in this moment so that I don't opt for the unhealthy choice?"

I know these are tough habits to break, but if I can do it, I also know you can do it! A few years ago, I scheduled a therapy session that I needed desperately. I was armed with a whole list of issues that were bothering me, and I was champing at the bit to share them with my therapist. But when I got there, I discovered that I'd written the date wrong on my calendar. My actual appointment was two days later. There I was, just bubbling over with problems to discuss with someone who would support me, and I couldn't let it all out.

I was stuck, but I didn't want to wallow in my habit of *not* supporting myself. With so many grievances right on the tip of my tongue, I could have gone down any number of negative roads in my head, including: "You're so stupid! You can't even get the appointment date right."

Instead, I asked myself a question: "If I had someone in my life who loved me unconditionally, what would I want them to do for me right now?" My answer was simple. I'd want them to take me to a particular luxe café in a nearby mall at Columbus

Circle in New York City. I'd want them to simply sit with me and relax while I read a book. Just that.

So what did I do? I took *myself* to that luxe café, and I sat there, giving myself unconditional love while I drank a delicious coffee and read my book.

At first, it can feel insufficient to give ourselves support rather than receive it from someone else, but the more you build your inner strength and love for yourself, the less your own support will feel like a consolation prize. The truth is that even when you accept support from someone else, it's a kind of self-support. That's because if you don't support yourself enough, you can't accept it from someone else. You can't let it in. It's the same with love. You can't accept or believe love from someone else unless you first love yourself.

When you learn how to give yourself the support you need, you feel instantly stronger. You know that you have an internal structure that provides you nourishment. This is a structure you can control and count on, while you can't control or always count on receiving nourishment and support from others. Yet, as I said before, I've found that the more support I offer myself, the more of it I receive from others because they reflect back to me what I'm carrying inside.

Journaling Exercise #15: Set Up Your Internal Support Structure

This exercise will help you begin to practice self-support in a new way, and it shouldn't take more than about 5 minutes to complete! But please write down your answers so that you can refer to them in moments when you're struggling to give yourself the support you need.

1. If someone who loves you unconditionally were here right now, what would you like him/her to do for you? Write it down! Can you do this for yourself in this moment? Even if it's a hug you want, you can wrap your arms around yourself and give yourself a hug.

2. If someone who loves you unconditionally were here right now, what would you like him/her to say to you? Write it down, and then read it out loud to yourself. You might feel strange at first, but let the words in as much as you can. Feel it! Then repeat it. Say it to yourself as many times as you want.
3. Over the next week or longer, say to yourself what you wrote down in number 2 whenever you think of it. If a day goes by, and you've forgotten to say it during your busy day, put a penny or paper clip in your pocket or use some other type of reminder. Every time you feel the reminder, say the unconditional words of encouragement to yourself. The more you say it, whether silent or out loud, the better.
4. The next time you feel a need for support, and there's no one available to ask, give yourself what you need. Do this especially when you're tempted to give yourself false support. Ask what you *truly* need, and do your best to provide it for yourself rather than going for the habitual, unhealthy choice.

MANTRA IN MOTION #6

Even if you feel you have little support from others right now, you can support *yourself* this very moment. Just take five minutes to reinforce your self-love and your trust in the support that's all around you. Doesn't it feel good to move your body while chanting a positive mantra? That's one of the best kinds of support there is!

Your Support Mantra

I release my doubts
It's all working out
Support is all around
I am breaking new ground!

Move 1: Chair Pose Release

Line 1: *I release my doubts*
Imagine letting go of all your doubts. As you perform this movement, try to feel a sense of surrender. As you lay down your doubts during this time, allow yourself to feel free of apprehension and fear.

"I release my doubts"

1. Start with your feet together, hands in prayer pose at your heart. Stand strong in this pose.
2. Lower to a chair pose and allow your arms to float out to the side. Let your palms face down toward the floor. Feel as though you are letting go of something and freeing your hands from holding on. As you lower yourself, say, "I release my . . ."
3. Rise back to starting position and say, ". . . doubts." As you bring your hands back together, feel a sense of peace. *This is one rep.*
4. Lower and rise for a total of 16 reps.

Move 2: Single Leg Balance

Line 2: *It's all working out*
This movement and mantra combination requires trust—trust that life is working on your behalf and that everything is aligning for your highest good. When you approach any challenge with the mind-set that it's all working out, you bring ease and faith to your actions.

"It's all working out"

1. Standing on your left leg, lift and bend your right knee so that your right foot comes to your left knee. You can also lift it just off the floor and hold it near your ankle.
2. Taking your time, slowly extend and straighten your right leg behind you, tilting your upper body over. Keep the core engaged. As you extend your leg, say, "It's all working . . ." Only tilt as far as you feel comfortable. It's not about how high you get your leg or how much you tilt, but rather that you are willing to take a risk and trust your body in the process.
3. Rise back to starting position and say, ". . . out." *This is one rep.*
4. Move through the two positions 8 times on one side and another 8 on the other leg.

Move 1: Chair Pose Release

Line 3: *Support is all around*
When we let ourselves feel supported by life, we begin to look for support in every direction. As you perform this move, be sure to engage your eyes. Look to the ground, look out in front of you, and maybe even turn your head to the left and right. Support is truly all around!

"Support is all around"

1. Start with your feet together, hands in prayer pose at your heart. Stand strong in this pose.
2. Lower to a chair pose and allow your arms to float out to the side. Let your palms face down toward the floor. Feel as though you are being supported as you move. As you lower yourself, say, "Support is all . . ."
3. Rise back to starting position and say, ". . . around." As you bring your hands back together, feel a sense of support. *This is one rep.*
4. Lower and rise for a total of 16 reps.

Move 2: Single Leg Balance

Line 4: *I am breaking new ground*
As you think about what it means to break new ground, call on the same trust you felt while doing this move the first time. Breaking new ground requires taking a risk. Are you willing to stand on one leg and take a risk, even if that might mean falling down? Go for it!

"I am breaking new ground"

1. Standing on your left leg, lift and bend your right knee so that your right foot comes to your left knee. You can also lift it just off the floor and hold it near your ankle.
2. Taking your time, slowly extend and straighten your right leg behind you, tilting your upper body over. Keep the core engaged. As you extend your leg, say, "I am breaking new . . ." Only tilt as far as you feel comfortable. Remember, it's not about how high you get your leg or how much you tilt, but rather that you are willing to take a risk.
3. Rise back to starting position and say, ". . . ground." *This is one rep.*
4. Move through the two positions 8 times on one side and another 8 on the other leg.

Putting It All Together

Now you're going to put the whole cycle together for 10 cycles. You will alternate between Move 1 and 2, but you'll do the right side with move 2 the first time through and the left side the second time through. So it will flow like this:

Move 1: Chair Pose Release
Mantra: *I release my doubt*
(As you come up, take a pause and then lift your right leg to your knee to start performing the next move.)

Move 2: Single Leg Balance
Mantra: *It's all working out*
(You will only do 1 rep, extending the right leg out. Then place the foot down, preparing for Move 1 again.)

Move 1: Chair Pose Release
Mantra: *Support is all around*
(As you come up, take a pause and then lift your left leg to your knee to start performing the next move.)

Move 2: Single Leg Balance
Mantra: *I am breaking new ground*
(You will only do 1 rep, extending the left leg out. Then place the foot down, preparing for Move 1 again.)
You will repeat this whole cycle 10 times.

CHAPTER 8

ALLOW AND ACCEPT WHAT IS

I once worked with an acting teacher who had coached Nicole Kidman for her Oscar-winning performance in the movie *The Hours*. This was a guy who knew what he was talking about, so I took his advice to heart.

He told me about the dangers of overacting, especially when you try to "act" qualities you already have naturally. "Erin, you're obviously intelligent, and as a dancer, you're very much 'in your body.' It's likely that every character you play in your career will come across as intelligent and strong," he said. "If you try too hard to make your character have those qualities, it will be too much."

Then I realized that overacting applies to more than just acting. It applies to our everyday lives too.

You'll recall our discussion of the difference between inspired action and an action that comes out of ego and fear. Inspired action feels good. Most of the time, it's fun, or at least it's exciting even if it scares us. *Inspired action comes out of the core of who we are.* We take action from our truth, which is what actors try to do in every single role. *Not over*acting. And whether we're on stage or in life, acting from truth is transformative. It wins Academy Awards for people like Nicole Kidman, and it helps the rest of us get out of our own way, be our true selves, and trust what's meant for us in this life.

But when our wishes don't come true immediately, trust is hard to come by. We doubt ourselves, and we push . . . *hard*. We try to force what we want to happen. As I said in Chapter 2, it's important to declare what we want and then let it go. It's just that letting it go is easier said than done.

Think back to puberty. (I know you don't want to—who does? But indulge me for just a minute.) Did you ever try too hard to get someone to like you? That seems to be true for all of us. You wanted *so much* for that person to like you, but the intense wanting might be exactly what got in the way.

Intense wanting can be an obstacle when we try to turn any of our desires into reality. Yes, we need to take action. It doesn't work to become a couch potato or adopt a do-nothing attitude. But the other extreme is also a problem.

In one of my classes, I gave each of my students a pot of soil and some seeds for daisies. I asked them to take the pot home, plant the seeds, and water the soil. When they came back the next week, I asked them, "Did any of you watch your pot during the week, thinking, 'Where are my darn daisies'?" Everybody laughed, of course, because nobody really expected results that fast. But the fact remains that we often get impatient when we're waiting for our desires.

Within a few weeks, those who continued to water their seeds began to see little buds coming through. But it certainly didn't happen because they pushed the seeds to grow faster. They simply needed to tend to the seeds and allow them to do their thing.

I experienced that when my husband and I were trying to conceive. After months of trying, I still wasn't pregnant. So I started to do everything I could to help my body along. I read books, got acupuncture, took supplements, and cleaned up my diet. Despite what I felt were my best efforts, I *still* wasn't pregnant after several more months passed by.

Not only did I become frustrated, but I also became aware that deep down, I was growing ambivalent about having a baby. Was it part of my core values to become a parent? Would I even be upset if we didn't manage to become parents? The more we struggled to conceive, the more my ambivalence grew. *Maybe it isn't meant to be,* I thought.

I think it's human nature to question what we truly want, when what we've thought we wanted hasn't shown up in a reasonable period of time. Ambivalence is normal and healthy, and I find it rears its head more strongly when we fear failure. To some degree, I believe it's a defense mechanism to protect us from disappointment.

Despite my ambivalence, my husband and I decided that we would reach out to a fertility doctor. After they performed a multitude of tests, it was clear that there were no glaring reasons for my not getting pregnant. We were now at a real crossroads. We could continue trying naturally or follow a fertility protocol. This was the moment that I had to look my ambivalence in the eye and determine what I truly wanted in my heart of hearts.

The fertility protocol felt like a bigger commitment toward becoming a parent. I would be saying, "Yes! This is definitely what I want, and I'm willing to do whatever it takes." At the same time, I had to temper my fear of failing, as I couldn't know if or when I would get pregnant.

After lots of thinking and talking, my husband and I decided to move forward with the support of our doctor. If you know anyone who has gone through fertility treatments or you have undergone them yourself, you know it can be an emotional road. You're forced to invite other people into a process that has always been private.

But I was determined to not be filled with fear and resentment during the process. I took the doctors' instructions with as much gratitude, joy, love, and faith as I could muster. Of course, this doesn't mean that I was perfectly happy and content all along the way. I allowed all my feelings to come up to the surface so that I could acknowledge and express them rather than hold them in.

But the journey was a huge lesson in allowing and letting go. I could be frustrated or anxious, or I could allow the divine timing of becoming a parent to unfold . . . or not. I chose to *allow* as best I could.

We were quite lucky that it didn't take long at all before I was pregnant with my little baby girl. Once she was in my arms, all my ambivalence was gone. As I write this, my new daughter is almost six months old, and I can't imagine my life without her! It was entirely worth the wait and every uncomfortable step we had to take.

Delays can have a wisdom of their own, even though they're frustrating. Sometimes they're exactly what we need to fine-tune our desires or maybe discover that we don't want what we thought we wanted. Someone else in my situation might have come to terms with not wanting a child after all.

What I learned is that when we're trying to create anything in life—whether it's a new job or a child—many elements have to come together at the same time. The wisdom of timing is so much more complex than we can possibly understand.

When we try to force what we want to come true before its time, we are resisting "what is"—the reality of the moment. If, on the other hand, we stop pushing so hard for what we want and trust in support from life, we begin to *allow* our life to unfold. When we move into flow and allowing, we're no longer contracted with fear that we won't get what we want. We trust that it's just a matter of time before we'll have what's rightfully ours.

You already have a natural desire to grow and expand. This longing to become "more" is pulsing through you, even when you sleep. There's no need to put sugar on top of sugar.

All we can do is plant the seeds and wait to see what comes, trusting that what's best for us will happen when it's right. In fact, let's start with this chapter's mantra:

What is for me cannot pass me
What is meant for me will arrive
Perfect people, perfect choices
Perfect opportunities in perfect time!

And again for good measure:

What is for me cannot pass me
What is meant for me will arrive
Perfect people, perfect choices
Perfect opportunities in perfect time!

Meditation #4: Learning to Allow and Accept What Is

This meditation will help you let go into an experience of allowing "what is." Sit in a comfortable chair where you won't be interrupted or distracted for 15 to 20 minutes.

You can record the meditation yourself and play it back, or you can visit my website for an audio version www.erinstutland.com/gifts. Just keep your eyes closed throughout the meditation (except when I suggest you open your eyes) so that you don't interrupt your relaxation.

1. Take a deep breath in. Exhale. Take another deep breath, and exhale. Pay attention to the rise and fall of your breath—the inhale and the exhale. The inhale and the exhale. If your mind starts to wander, just continue to bring it back to the rise and fall of your breath.
2. Notice that your breathing happens automatically. All you have to do is allow it. No matter what you think or believe in this moment, the breath still happens. It's almost as if your body is breathing you. It's effortless and easy.
3. Turn your attention to the beating of your heart. Your heart beats regardless of what you think, believe, or do. It is automatic and effortless.
4. Touch the fabric of the clothing you're wearing. Is it smooth or textured? Marvel in the fact that your hands can feel it without forcing anything. You don't have to make yourself feel it. It just happens.
5. You have an innate faith in these functions of your body, trusting that they'll support you. You take them for granted. They come so easily to you because they've been a natural part of your life since you were a baby. But what if you were to extend that faith and trust to all parts of your life? Think about the support that life provides you. How would it feel if you trusted that life supports you and your desires even while you sleep?

6. Your life is like a raft floating on the water. Imagine the river flowing fast and that opportunities are coming your way that are beyond what your mind could ever conceive. Now imagine the river flowing so slowly that it feels like you aren't going anywhere, and no opportunities seem to come. What if, in these slower moments, you could have the same kind of faith that you have in the beating of your heart and the breathing of your lungs? Imagine what it would feel like to have that kind of faith—to trust unequivocally that life supports you. That you don't have to make your desires happen through blood, sweat, and tears. That you can trust the seeds you've planted. That you can believe life has your back.
7. Think about your life as it is right now. If you aren't satisfied with everything, what would it feel like to accept it all *as it is*? Imagine that you trust life so implicitly that regardless of the challenges you face, you accept your job, family, friends, finances, body, and circumstances as they are. In this moment, even if it's just for a moment, allow it to be "all good." Let out a big exhale that releases the need to change anything—just for now. Allow yourself to have the experience of accepting what is.
8. As you read the next words, repeat them in your mind or aloud, whichever you prefer. *"I simply show up. I stay the course. I'm always connected in each and every moment to infinite source. I am enough. I have enough. I do enough every single day. I now claim that what is for me cannot and will not pass by me. What's meant for me will arrive—the perfect people, the perfect opportunities, and the perfect choices—in the perfect time."*
9. Imagine that your heart is opening like a flower blooming toward the sun. That flower receives the sunlight without thinking for a moment, "I don't deserve this light" or "what if I don't manage to bloom?" Your heart is now a flower that accepts

all life wants to offer you. It opens to receiving all that you want. Life responds to what you want with either "yes," "not right now," or "here's something better." Trust and allow that!

10. Let's repeat these words again. You can think them or say them to yourself in a whisper: *"I simply show up. I stay the course. I'm always connected in each and every moment to infinite source. I am enough. I have enough. I do enough every single day. I now claim that what is for me cannot and will not pass by me. What's meant for me will arrive—the perfect people, the perfect opportunities, and the perfect choices—in the perfect time."*
11. Take a final deep breath in, bow your head forward, and exhale all your breath out. When you're ready, open your eyes, and know that you're allowing what you want to come your way in the proper time.

Acceptance vs. Settling

Not long ago, I got a juicy question from one of my followers. A few days later, the same question arrived from five more people! They wondered: *If I accept and love myself as I am—my being, my body, and my life—am I settling? Does that mean I no longer want more? Is it possible that self-acceptance is just a way of throwing in the towel and saying, "Screw it; I'm done trying"?*

These are valid questions. How do you balance a sense of gratitude for what you already have with your desire for more in your life? How do you accept "what is" and still strive for a better life?

To answer this, let's talk first about the energy of "settling." I grew up with a wonderful, fierce mom who was a master at inflicting Jewish guilt (although I know Jewish moms hardly have a monopoly on guilt). When I was a teen, I was stubborn. I would push and push until she'd finally give in. "Fine!" she'd say in resignation. "Do what you want then!"

I wanted her approval, and I wanted her to let me do what I wanted. But her subtext was, "I'm tired of fighting with you, and I'm giving up. I'm just not happy about it."

That's what settling feels like. It involves giving up because we're sick of trying. There's a thread of anger and deep disappointment underneath it.

Allowing and acceptance have a very different energy. Acceptance of who you are in this moment doesn't mean you don't care anymore. It simply means you embrace the truth of *what is* in this moment, the truth of who you are and what you have—even if you aren't totally satisfied. You appreciate all you've done to get where you are today, and you embrace all your feelings, from gratitude to frustration. You allow and accept all of it!

There's a sweetness to acceptance. It's an act of unconditional love. But not for a second does it negate the desire for expansion, for more, or for better.

We accept our friends as they are, while encouraging them to strive for more. Why is it so difficult to do this for ourselves? My client Bree came to realize she needed to treat herself just like she treated her best friends. "I accept and allow them to be themselves, and I love them regardless. I decided to make myself my own best friend and speak to myself with the same kindness and compassion that I use when talking to someone I love. The greatest gift of allowing is the unconditional love that I feel right now for myself, even if I'm not quite where I'd like to be."

It's a paradox to accept where we are at this moment while also wanting more. It brings to mind the serenity prayer: "God grant me the serenity to accept the things I cannot change, the courage to change the things I can, and the wisdom to know the difference."

How do you truly accept the now and maintain the energy of wanting more at the same time? Let's explore that from an energetic perspective, but first, let's revisit our mantra.

What is for me cannot pass me
What is meant for me will arrive
Perfect people, perfect choices
Perfect opportunities in perfect time!

Karen's Story

My client Karen made a profound journey from self-hatred to self-acceptance. "I spent all of my teens and most of my twenties judging myself and working to 'fix' what I felt was wrong with me. Then I'd hate myself for not being 'good enough,'" she says. "When I started having serious feelings for one of my long-time friends, I felt I couldn't date him until I lost weight and finished my stint with adult braces. I couldn't accept myself the way I was, so how could he? But eventually, I couldn't deny my feelings, so I allowed the relationship to flow naturally from friendship to romance. I started using the mantra 'I accept myself exactly as I am,' which I didn't believe at all at the time. Then, before long, I began to notice that I felt more comfortable in my own skin. Through developing that love of myself, my friend turned boyfriend was able to see all there is to love about me and not be pushed away by my negative opinions of myself. Through building my self-acceptance of who I was in the moment, I became the woman I've always wanted to be and am still in the process of becoming. That sweet man is now my beloved husband, and when he tells me why he loves me, I allow it to sink in completely and accept it as truth. I learned to accept myself as I am right now. This has allowed me to have experiences I never would have had, take chances and risks, explore life more, and love myself and others so much more deeply. I'm no longer waiting to live my life. I'm living it and loving it!"

Meditation #5: Accept without Settling

This isn't technically a meditation, but it helps if you close your eyes. Try this whenever you get confused about accepting who you are right now while still wanting more. It only takes a couple of minutes to do, but it's powerful.

1. Place one hand on your heart. (It doesn't matter which hand.) Think about what you're grateful for in this moment. If you struggle to think of something to be grateful for, remember that you have a roof over your head, food to eat, and the ability to read this book right now.
2. Extend your other arm out in front of you with your palm up in the pose of openness and receptivity. Say to yourself silently or aloud, "I'm grateful for what I have, and I'm also open, willing, able, and ready to receive more." Repeat it as many times as you like.
3. Open your eyes, and trust that you can accept yourself right now and still receive what you want in the future.

The Yin and Yang of Ease

My friend and acupuncturist Deb Ross once told me that *chi* (sometimes spelled *qi*), or our life force or energy, flows freely through our bodies like a river. But just like a river might stop flowing when a tree falls in its way, we experience blocks to the flow of our chi. Our emotional and physical traumas, negative beliefs and thoughts, and pushing too hard for what we want can all become trees in the river of our chi.

"Chi circulates through the body and mind. When there's a disruptive thought or an injury, the chi flow is interrupted," Deb says. "This interruption can either be moved or balanced quickly, or it can become something more significant over time. Often, we're stuck too much in thought and not in our feelings. These mental blocks don't allow us to see the truth about ourselves, certain relationships, or old wounds. We might think it's easier to be in pain than to feel deep sadness or anger. But we have to feel feelings. We can't think feelings."

When we *allow* (there's that word again) our feelings to move through, the block (the proverbial tree over the river) is removed so that the chi can flow again. (If you find it very difficult to connect with your emotions, I highly recommend seeing a therapist if at all possible.)

The free flow of our chi also requires a balance between yin and yang energies. In simple terms, yang energy refers to movement, while yin energy refers to stillness. Deb says that in today's society, we tend to run around and live our lives too outwardly with little time for stillness. We're starved for yin activities like meditation, nature walks, breathing exercises, qigong, tai chi, yoga, and gentle movement. Yang activities like physical exercise and running errands are much more common in our society. But the more balance we have in our lives between yin and yang activities, the better our chi flows, and the easier it is to allow and accept what comes in and out of our lives.

The problem is that creating what we want requires very active yang energy. Allowing and accepting, on the other hand, require the yin energy of stillness. It's a big energetic balancing act that requires us to have flexibility while we work on creating our desires and then letting them go.

Resistance comes into play because we don't want to stop the yang energy of trying to make it happen. It feels good to keep pushing—to "overact," so to speak—because we feel more in control. When we move into the yin energy of allowing, we relinquish control. That can cause us to feel scared and defeated.

"Allowing is about guiding yourself to your heart, to the center in your body," Deb says, "and trusting what happens as each moment unfolds."

It's a kind of surrender, but it doesn't mean giving up. It means taking a deep breath and allowing for the possibility that what you want could come easily. Maybe, just maybe it doesn't have to be so hard to get what you want. Have you ever thought of that?

I can't deny that I've watched many of my clients get what they want as soon as they surrendered and stopped trying so hard. It isn't that they stopped wanting. They just stopped obsessing about the seeds they'd planted. After all, when you plant a garden, you don't plant the seeds every day, do you? You plant them once, and you wait, *allowing* them to grow when they do. Meanwhile, you get on with your life and enjoy yourself as much as you can!

How can you enjoy your life when you don't have what you want? You make the most of what you *do* have. If you want a romantic partner more than anything, find ways to enjoy your friends and your own company. If you hate your job, find ways to have fun during your off time until a better job comes along. If you're low in funds, look for ways to experience joy without spending money. But in the meantime, it's all about planting your seeds, trusting that they'll grow, and getting on with your life.

Balance between relaxing and enjoying the moment—and working on yourself is the key. Balance, of course, is an ideal that we rarely achieve 100 percent of the time. When surrender feels impossible, revisit the allowing meditation earlier in the chapter. It will help you trust that your desire is already living and breathing through you. It will help you trust that the actions you take are enough, and you'll move closer to balance.

You can also take a deep breath and simply say, "Easy!" whenever you feel yourself worrying that your dreams won't come true. In this instance, the word has a double meaning—to calm you down and also to affirm that what you desire will come to you without struggle.

Simply do your best to strike what feels like a balance within yourself of the yin and the yang. When you feel yourself pushing toward a desire, you'll probably feel tension somewhere in your body or mind. You might even feel a bit of desperation. After all, you want it *so much*.

That's exactly the moment to say, "Easy!" to yourself and maybe take that walk in nature. Talk to yourself about trusting that the seeds have been planted. Then maybe sometime down the road, you'll begin to feel that it's time to take yang action again. But as you work on your personal version of balance, you'll begin to get a better sense of when to push forward and when to slow down.

Now let's do a journaling exercise that will show you even more what it means to surrender the seeds you've planted to the Universe—to life.

Journaling Exercise #16: Your Universe Jar

Life has your best interests at heart. Are you willing to acknowledge your constant connection to the Universe—the divine source—believing that it has the power to work out the details of what you want beyond your conscious mind's capacity? Let's see what happens when you do that.

1. Set aside 15 minutes for this exercise.
2. Visit www.erinstutland.com/gifts, and print the Universe Jar sheet. Or you can simply cut a piece of paper into 12 or so pieces.
3. Choose a desire you've been working toward—one for which you believe you've done all the work you can. In the individual boxes, write down all your fears, worries, doubts, and concerns about creating this desire.
4. Use scissors to cut the squares along the dotted lines.
5. Find a box or jar, and label it "Universe Jar," "Universe Box," or whatever word you prefer for higher power, such as Life, God, Krishna, Buddha, etc.
6. Say out loud, "Any concern I put in this container will be taken care of by a force greater than I can imagine. It's no longer mine to worry about. I won't think about it anymore or try to figure it out. I trust that the Universe will take care of this for me."
7. Put all the pieces of paper in the container, and put it on a shelf or in a drawer. Then go do something fun! Enjoy the moment.
8. Knowing that you have let go, trust that you've planted the perfect seeds and that your desires will blossom in divine timing.

MANTRA IN MOTION #7

Allowing and accepting what is can be difficult. Let's make it easier by moving your body as you affirm that what is for you cannot pass you. "Allow" this workout to be meditative for you. Trust and feel at ease!

Your Allow and Accept Mantra
What is for me cannot pass me
What is meant for me will arrive
Perfect people, perfect choices
Perfect opportunities in perfect time!

Move 1: Single Leg Lunge

Line 1: *What is for me cannot pass me*
Move into a state of allowing while trusting that what is meant to be in your life most certainly will, without you having to push or make it happen.

"What is for me cannot pass me"

1. Start with your feet together and your hands in prayer pose at your heart. Stand strong in this pose.
2. Step your right leg back into a lunge, bending both knees. Be sure to track your left knee directly over your left ankle. Bring your hands down to a *V* position. As you step back, say, "What is for me . . ."
3. Step your feet back together and pause. Breathe.
4. Step your left leg back to a lunge on the other side and say, ". . . cannot pass me."
5. Step your feet back together and breathe. *This is one rep.* You will do this whole thing through 8 times.

Move 2: Side Lunge

Line 2: *What is meant for me will arrive*
This mantra will help you to trust the timing of life, knowing that it is not always in your control, but that what is meant for you will come at the perfect time. This doesn't mean you stop trying or completely leave it up to fate. It simply means that you take your actions from a place of ease and faith.

"What is meant for me will arrive"

1. Begin with your feet together and hands in prayer pose.
2. Keeping your toes pointing forward, step out to your right, bending your right leg but keeping your left leg straight. You are in a lateral lunge. Be sure that your right knee tracks right over your right toe. As you lunge, say, "What is meant . . ."
3. Push off your right leg, bringing it back to the starting position. As you do so, say, ". . . for me. . ."
4. Step out to the other side and perform the lunge with the left leg. As you lunge out, say, ". . . will arrive."
5. Step your foot back into the starting position, pause, and breathe. Moving right to left is one rep. You will repeat this mantra 8 times, so you will essentially be doing 16 lunges, 8 on each side.

Move 1: Single Leg Lunge

Line 3: *Perfect people, perfect choices*
Have you ever been partnered with someone for a project and thought, *Why did I end up with this person?* Imagine if instead, you thought, *Wow, this is the perfect person to be paired with.* I invite you to approach all the people you meet and the choices that you make as though they are absolutely perfect for where you are right now.

"Perfect people, perfect choices"

1. Start with your feet together and your hands in prayer pose at your heart. Stand strong in this pose.
2. Step your right leg back into a lunge, bending both knees. Be sure to track your left knee directly over your left ankle. Bring your hands down to a *V* position. As you step back, say, "Perfect people . . ."
3. Step your feet back together and pause. Breathe.
4. Step your left leg back to a lunge on the other side and say, ". . . perfect choices."
5. Step your feet back together and breathe. *This is one rep.* You will do this whole thing through 8 times.

Move 2: Side Lunge

Line 4: *Perfect opportunities in perfect time*
Continuing on from the last mantra, every opportunity that comes your way is the perfect one for your growth and well-being, and they all happen in perfect timing!

"Perfect opportunities in perfect time"

1. Begin with your feet together and your hands by your side.
2. Keeping your toes pointing forward, step out to your right, bending your right leg but keeping your left leg straight. You are in a lateral lunge. Be sure that your right knee tracks right over your right toe. As you lunge, say, "Perfect opportunities . . ."
3. Push off your right leg, bringing it back to the starting position. Pause and breathe.
4. Step out to the other side and perform the lunge with the left leg. As you lunge out, say, ". . . in perfect time."
5. Step your foot back into the starting position, pause, and breathe. Moving right to left is one rep. You will repeat this mantra 8 times, so you will essentially be doing 16 lunges, 8 on each side.

Putting It All Together

Now you are going to put the *whole* thing together for 10 cycles. Alternate between Move 1 and Move 2. So it will flow like this:

> Move 1: Single Leg Lunge
> Mantra: *What is for me cannot pass me*
> *(Lunge back on the right and left leg. Then bring your feet together, ready for the next move.)*
>
> Move 2: Side Lunge
> Mantra: *What is meant for me will arrive*
> *(Lunge to the right and left. You will be in the perfect position to return to the back lunges.)*
>
> Move 1: Single Leg Lunge
> Mantra: *Perfect people, perfect choices*
> *(Lunge back on the right and left leg, then prepare for your side lunge.)*
>
> Move 2: Side Lunge
> Mantra: *Perfect opportunities in perfect time*
> *(After lunging to the side right and left, you have completed one cycle.)*
> *You will repeat this whole cycle 10 times.*

CHAPTER 9

MAKE SPACE FOR GREATNESS

I visited New York City for the first time when I was 16 years old, and from then on, my dream was to live in the East Village—a hip, grungy, artist-filled part of town. It had cafés, open-mic nights, street performers, and vintage shops—the ultimate playground for a wide-eyed artist ready to take on the world.

After living on the Upper East Side during my first year after college, I was finally able to scrounge together enough money to get a tiny studio smack dab in the middle of the East Village. The apartment was in a former tenement building and was a whopping 250 square feet. There was a wardrobe but no closets and just enough space for a bed and small seating area. The bathroom had a stand-up shower and a toilet. No sink, and no bathtub. This meant I had to wash my dishes, my face, and my teeth in the kitchen sink. With paper-thin walls, I could hear every move my neighbors made, including the rotating parade of women my upstairs neighbor brought home. Sounds idyllic, doesn't it?

Yet, despite the fact that it was probably a parent's nightmare for their daughter, it was everything I wanted. I finally felt like I was in the epicenter of the creative universe and had inspiration at my fingertips every day.

But over time, my Bohemian fantasy began to wear thin. The apartment wasn't so comfortable, so maybe I was ready to grow up a bit.

A friend told me about a program in which 20 percent of the units in new, luxury, doorman buildings in the neighborhood of Chelsea (a bit northwest of the East Village) were being subsidized by the city so that the developer could earn a tax break. The units would be available to people who fell within a low-income bracket. I was barely making ends meet with odds-and-ends jobs, so I was a perfect candidate!

The apartment would have a landscaped roof deck, a washer/dryer, and lots of light compared to my dark tenement. Plus, the building had a gym and 24-hour concierge service! But the best part was I'd pay a small fraction of what I was paying for my tenement studio. Amazing, right?

The application process was arduous, and I learned that it might take several months or even years before I got a place. Still, why not throw my name in the hat and see what happened? Every month, I gathered my paperwork and sent it to my case worker in order to stay on top of the process. But eventually, I became a bit careless about keeping up with my paperwork. I began to feel a deep inner conflict about moving to the luxury building.

Now, before you think I'm crazy, let me explain. I was so used to my neighborhood, my way of life, and even my struggle, that a part of me thought I would lose my identity by moving to the posh location. Who would I be if I wasn't a struggling artist? Would people think I was rich, snobby, and in no way a true creative? Would I still feel connected to inspiration and the deep longing that comes from not ever getting what you want? Talk about a limited belief! But at the time, a part of me wanted to stay safe exactly where I was.

Then an older friend of mine, who was a talented and successful music producer, set me straight. He was making an excellent living in the business, and he was one of the most creative people I knew. "Erin, you have to make room for greatness," he told me. "You're more than just a struggling artist. You want to make a living doing what you love. You want to thrive and live in a beautiful home that allows you to explore your creativity without financial pressure. Moving into this new apartment *will* change your life, but for the better. You'll see what it's like to live in a place that feels 'rich.' It will allow you to grow into the person you long to become."

He was absolutely right. I was afraid of change and stuck in small thinking. If I stayed in my tiny studio and denied myself this new opportunity, I wouldn't create space for greatness in my life.

So right after that talk with my music-producer friend, I walked to the luxury building and envisioned myself stepping inside, greeting the doormen, strolling through the neighborhood, and getting on the subway at the nearest station. Every night from then on, I visualized myself living in that new apartment, even to the point that I saw myself standing over an actual *bathroom sink* brushing my teeth!

It took a few months, but the call from my case worker finally came. Yes, I'd be moving into one of those units! I felt like I'd won the lottery, and it became one of the defining moments of my 20s.

Moving into that apartment did indeed change my life for the better. By shifting my thinking and allowing space for change—for a greater and better reality—I was able to step into a new version of myself. Having less financial overhead allowed me to explore new options for work instead of taking whatever was available to pay my bills. I got my real estate license, which helped me make more money than I'd ever made, while still having the flexibility to go to auditions. It allowed me to become bicoastal, traveling back and forth between New York and Los Angeles for acting gigs. I'd never been able to afford to do that before.

Plus, coming home to that beautiful space made me feel rich. Even though I was paying a lot less than the average rent in the building, I was living among some of the wealthiest people in Manhattan. Money is far from everything, but it reinforced in me the ability to create more abundance in my life.

The "moral" of this story is: we have to literally create the space for our dreams to manifest—in our physical world, in our minds, and in our hearts. That's what we're going to explore in this chapter.

So what's our mantra? Here you go:

I make space for greatness
I call in my success
I am powerful
I attract the very best!

Read it again because it's a powerful declaration:

I make space for greatness
I call in my success
I am powerful
I attract the very best!

How Being Tidy Helps You Create What You Want

My friend Ellen admits she can be a bit messy. A few years ago, she was very busy as she prepared to go away to a meditation retreat. There just wasn't time to clean her apartment before she had to leave.

While at the retreat, she slowed down, calmed her mind, and returned home feeling content and serene. But when she opened the door to her apartment, the chaotic mess was like a slap in the face. That environment didn't match how she felt after meditating in nature. She hated it enough that ever since, she makes sure her home is clean and orderly before she goes on a trip.

Have you ever had that experience? You evolve and suddenly discover that something in your life no longer "matches" the person you've become? That's part of what it means to make space for greatness.

But even if you haven't yet changed on the inside the way you want, you can begin to speed up that inner transformation by matching your outer world to the person you want to become.

Of course, I'm not talking about making yourself into someone you're not. I'm talking about staying true to yourself as you reach for your greater potential.

I experienced this when I went through a bit of my own neatness renaissance. Even though I love to clean and love a clean home, I'd hardly consider myself naturally tidy. For years, cleaning was a cycle like this: I'd make everything look beautifully spotless. Then, within two to four days, everything would be a mess again.

I even had a running joke about it with my husband via text message:

Me: Love, oh my goodness, I think someone broke into the apartment!

Him: What?!

Me: Yeah, I came home, and there were clothes and shoes absolutely everywhere! I can hardly see the floor. We definitely had robbers. I don't think they took anything, but they made a huge mess!

Him: Love, did you make a mess today?

Me: Yes, I'm so sorry. Don't hate me. [prayer emoji] I promise to clean it up.

Let's just say we had "robbers" more often than I'd like to admit. At some point, though, I accepted the cycle of cleanup, followed quickly by mess.

Then I read Marie Kondo's book *The Life-Changing Magic of Tidying Up*. It turned me into someone who strives to keep our apartment tidy on an ongoing basis, which is nothing short of miraculous. Not a single robber has paid a visit since, and our home continuously maintains a feeling of calmness and peace, which helps me to stay calmer and more peaceful on the inside.

Plus, Kondo's book goes beyond the external appearance of your home and asks you to discard whatever fails to bring you joy—not what gave you joy in the past, but what provides joy to the person you are now.

I'd always been told that we should release impractical objects that are no longer useful. But I think releasing what doesn't bring us joy makes a lot more sense.

In fact, I would even take it one step further: What items will bring joy to the person you're striving to become? In other words, in order to say yes to what we want, we have to say no to what we don't want. For example, I had to give up the idea that struggle is part of being an artist. I had to give up some articles of clothing that no longer matched my vision for myself. I had to tell my girlfriend that she wasn't allowed to speak to me disrespectfully anymore. Most every yes to the new is a no to the old.

Let's say you have an outfit that you once loved, but it reminds you of a painful event in your life. Maybe you have a vase that an ex-partner gave you. While you might like the vase, seeing it reminds you of the way that person treated you, which was less than respectful. What about the beautiful suit you wore at the job you hated, where your boss fired you? The shirt you wore when you had a poor self-image?

Sometimes, we hold on to objects because we simply haven't thought about how they don't fit the person we've become or who we want to be. It's a habit to keep them. We're so accustomed to the way our lives have been that we don't even notice how much our environment no longer matches our new self. Like the raggedy towels we simply haven't bothered to replace. That was the case with my friend Valerie.

She grew up in a family that had to scrimp and save a lot of the time. Until she was an adult, she'd only owned fake-leather purses and polyester sheets. It had become so habitual for her to buy such things that even after she was making enough money for the occasional leather bag and high-thread-count sheets, she didn't buy them. It took a while for it to dawn on her that she could step out of the programming from her childhood and treat herself if she chose. She didn't spend hundreds of dollars either. She stayed within her budget while allowing her mindset to stretch into the person she was capable of being.

The point, of course, is not necessarily to spend money. I don't want anyone to feel bad if they can't afford a leather bag or luxurious sheets. Obviously, if your living room curtains don't bring you joy, but you can't afford to replace them yet, you'll keep them awhile longer. If you hate almost every item of clothing in your closet, I don't expect you to throw it all out. But as you become aware that so much of what you own is for the *old you* and not the *you of the future*, you'll begin to create the space for the new to come into your life. Then you can gradually discard the old as your budget allows.

In the meantime, you can find ways to fill your environment with more objects that bring you joy. If you have a few bucks, visit thrift stores until you find an affordable item you love. Make it like a treasure hunt! If you need a new suit for a job or interview, check those same thrift shops or take a look on eBay. In fact, when you're ready to replace those living-room curtains, you just might find the ones you want for a reduced price on eBay or through using online promotional codes. If you use your creativity, you can begin to surround yourself with what you love without going into debt.

As you let go of items that no longer bring you joy or match the person you're becoming, thank them for serving you. At one time, this object may have been perfect for you.

This process also gave me a new appreciation for what I chose to keep and caused me to take better care of what I own. As a result, I say thank you to my skirt for allowing a cool breeze to reach my legs on a hot day. I thank my bag for carrying my computer as I bounce around the city. I thank my winter boots for keeping my feet warm and dry in the snow.

There was another benefit for me: my newfound appreciation meant putting each item in its proper place *with pleasure*. As Marie Kondo says, "If you were at the bottom of a pile with a bunch of things stacked on you, how would you feel?" She says that because piles don't allow us to see all our items, we're less likely to use them. So I adopted her idea of folding clothes into vertical piles. This way, each piece has its own "slot" in my closet or drawer, which makes it easy to see where it is and easy to remove without making a mess. This kind of organization helps me to create a feeling of peace in my household.

Look around your home. Does your environment reflect the person you want to be? If you want more peace, it's up to you to keep your living space tidy and calm. If you have kids who constantly leave a mess, at least find one space for yourself (even if it's just a corner) where you can have the peace you want.

Go through your closets and cabinets. What doesn't fit with your vision for the future? What can you part with to make room for the greatness that's coming your way?

This is a perfect time to revisit our mantra:

I make space for greatness
I call in my success
I am powerful
I attract the very best!

Meditation #6: Step Outside the Box

It can be difficult to let go of our habitual way of being. We want to expand and grow, but we become stuck in what's familiar. Let's step into the new you right now. This is a short meditation that should only take 5 to 10 minutes.

You can record the meditation yourself and play it back, or you can visit my website for an audio version at www.erinstutland.com/gifts. Just keep your eyes closed throughout so that you don't interrupt your relaxation.

1. Take a deep breath in. Exhale. Take another deep breath, and exhale. Pay attention to the rise and fall of your breath—the inhale and the exhale. The inhale and the exhale. Repeat this 5 times. If your mind starts to wander, gently bring it back to focusing on your breath.
2. Imagine that you're sitting inside a box. (Make it large enough that you don't feel claustrophobic.) This box represents your familiar way of being—the way you're accustomed to living your life right now.
3. In order to make room for the greatness that you're destined for, imagine that you break open this box and step outside of it. Push down those walls, and feel the freedom of being outside of your self-imposed confines.
4. The world is your oyster. Feel all the possibilities available to you now that you're no longer constricted by your habitual box. Breathe in all that life has to offer you. What will you do with this

vast space and opportunity? Allow yourself to feel excited for your future. *Believe in your ability to make room for greatness.*

Make Room on the Inside Too!

Have you ever seen the movie *Bridesmaids*? It's one of many movies in which the main character (in this case, played by Kristen Wiig) is involved with a less-than-respectful romantic partner (played by Jon Hamm). He even tells her at one point that she's his "number three" girl. Throughout the course of the film, Wiig's character gradually develops enough self-esteem to realize she deserves better, and she finally tells Hamm's character to take a hike.

What about you? Has your life ever changed for the better because you developed yourself enough to stretch beyond what you previously believed you deserved? How are you different now than before your life improved? Did your comfort zone expand? Did you learn to believe in yourself more? I'll bet if you think about it, there's at least one way during the course of your life that you progressed because your mind-set changed. The good news is that you can do that again, and we're going to explore how.

As we make room for greatness in our environment, we can make room on the inside as well. Otherwise, we might not be ready emotionally for what comes our way. How often have we heard stories of people who win the lottery or become a huge success in the music or film business, only to end up bankrupt again? Sometimes the time we wait for our desire is time we need to prepare ourselves for what's coming.

One of the key ways you can prepare yourself for the greatness that's on its way is to live "as if" it's already true. This is like the play acting we did as children. You step into the role of who you want to be, which gets your psyche ready for the new reality. If you want abundance, you begin to feel what it's like to have money, sort of like I did when I moved into that luxury building. If you want more self-confidence, you begin to act as though you already have it. If you want a promotion, you begin to act (quietly in your mind, of course) like you're already in the position.

Playing the role also makes you attract what you want. Your subconscious mind doesn't know the difference between reality and play acting, so living "as if" helps your outer world to begin to match the way you feel on the inside.

To live "as if," you may need to step out of your comfort zone. I know that can be scary, but it's an important step in creating that sweet life you want. If you desire a romantic partner, for example, how can you make room in your life for a relationship? Maybe you work all the time and need to be more social, letting the Universe know that you'll make time for someone to come into your life. Maybe you need to open up more to friends and become comfortable with deeper levels of intimacy.

If you want a better job, you might join a meet-up group with people who do the kind of work you'd like to do (even if you stay in the corner and don't speak to anyone at first). A friend of mine once audited a master class with one of her idols just so that she could be in the presence of someone with that level of talent. She didn't speak to a soul, but she absorbed the energy.

If you want to be a comedian, hang out where the successful comedians are. If you want to be an executive who makes a six-figure salary, walk into a department store and try on designer suits. If you want to travel the world and stay at five-star hotels, sit in the lobby of one of those hotels whenever you get the chance. Do whatever you can to begin to take on the role of this future you.

Just as you stepped out of the box in the earlier meditation, you have to step out of your comfort zone in order to reach your potential. And just as you got rid of objects in your home that no longer bring you joy or match the person you're becoming, you have to clear out internal issues that no longer serve you.

Of course, we've done a lot of that already, especially when we worked on releasing limiting beliefs. But what about other emotional loose ends that might be taking up valuable space in your internal world?

Anger is often one of those emotional loose ends, which brings me to the topic of forgiveness. When someone hurts us, the energy of that resentment can become an obstacle to creating what you want. Of course, you have to work yourself gently through the forgiveness process in your own time. You can't bypass your anger or pretend it away. But I believe it's important to continue to work toward releasing the resentment. Grudges take up real estate in our subconscious mind, our hearts, and our bodies.

If you're struggling to forgive someone, imagine talking with that person on the last day of his/her life. That can help to soften the anger and get it out so that the space it's taking up inside you is finally freed.

Guilt is another loose end that takes up space in the psyche. Where in your life do you feel you don't deserve greatness because you haven't made amends with someone? If that's the case, it's time to say you're sorry. If you no longer know how to reach the person involved, imagine a conversation in which you have a chance to apologize to that person. Then affirm to yourself that it's done by saying out loud, "I release myself from this guilt. It is done." If it helps you to feel better, make amends to someone by paying it forward—perform a random act of kindness as a way of saying you're sorry to the person you can't speak to directly.

With that in mind, let's remember our mantra:

I make space for greatness
I call in my success
I am powerful
I attract the very best!

Meditation #7: Make Room for the Future You

In this 15-minute meditation, you'll make some internal space for the future you to emerge, and you'll actually meet with that future you and ask questions that might give you valuable insights. Take your time with each step of this meditation, and allow yourself the space to explore each of the elements.

1. Close your eyes, and begin to relax each part of your body, starting with your feet and legs and moving up to your torso, chest, arms, shoulders, neck, head, and face. You don't even have to know how to relax your body. Just tell yourself each part is relaxing.
2. Think of someone you need to forgive—someone who has wronged you. Imagine that your anger is a big ball of churning red smoke in your solar plexus. It's taking up a lot of space. Take that ball of red smoke, and place it in the basket of a hot-air balloon. By putting it in the balloon, you're not condoning whatever the other person did. You're simply freeing yourself of the anger and hurt. Go ahead and give the balloon a push, and watch it fly up into the air farther and farther away until you can't see it anymore. Feel the room you've made in the center of your body as a result of releasing that red ball of smoke. This is free, peaceful space now.
3. Think of someone *you've* wronged—something you feel guilty about. Imagine that the guilt is a dark cloud of smoke over your heart that prevents you from loving yourself as fully as you could. Take that dark cloud, and put it into the basket of another hot-air balloon. Give this balloon a push as well, and allow it to fly up and up until it's out of your sight. Once again, feel the space you've made in your heart. There's so much more love available to you now.

4. Think about a time in your life when you received something out of nowhere. Maybe it was a gift you wanted, an award, or a compliment from someone that you didn't expect. Somewhere inside you, perhaps outside of your awareness, you made internal space for receiving this gift or compliment. Envision making space internally for more to come. Take a deep breath right now, and exhale anything extraneous. Exhale all that you don't need. You don't have to know what it is. Just trust that you're making internal space for positive change. Your cells and the space between your cells are open to changing for the better and receiving whatever beauty, love, and fun that life has to offer you. Know that you have infinite space inside you to create what you want and to be who you want to be.
5. Let's explore your future. Think about what you want your life to be like in two years. What will be different from the way it is now? Ask yourself: "What kind of person would I have to be to have the life I want in two years?" Picture yourself as a person with those qualities. See or feel the presence of this future you in front of you. Let's have a conversation with this future version of you.
6. Ask this future you from two years from now: "What do you want me to know about the future? How can I prepare for the new life I'm stepping into? Is there anything I need to do differently?" Listen carefully for the answers.
7. Let's project forward by five years. What will be different from the way it is now? Ask yourself: "What kind of person would I have to be to have the life I want in five years?" Picture yourself as a person with those qualities. See or feel the presence of this future you in front of you. Let's have a conversation with this future version of you.

8. Ask this future you from five years from now: "What do you want me to know about the future? How can I prepare for the new life I'm stepping into? Is there anything I need to do differently?" Listen carefully for the answers.
9. If you like, you can continue this exploration further into the future.
10. When you're ready, open your eyes, and write down what you recall that your future selves told you. Take any advice to heart, applying it to your plan for making room for greatness. What will you do with all the space you've just created for greatness to come in?

MANTRA IN MOTION #8

Call in your success and your power by moving your body. Remember: movement in your body creates movement in your life. Make the space and time for five minutes (or more) of greatness right now. Don't wait! It's how you'll attract the very best into your life.

Your Make Space for Greatness Mantra

I make space for greatness
I call in my success
I am powerful
I attract the very best!

Move 1: Jumping Jack or Modified Jumping Jack

Line 1: *I make space for greatness*
Greatness can't come through unless we make space for it—mind, body, and spirit. What will it take for you to create more room for what you want, particularly if that means feeling good?

"I make space for greatness"

1. Start with your feet together, hands by your side. Jump your legs out to hips' distance apart as you bring your arms above your head, then jump your feet back together and bring your arms down. Say, "I make space for . . ."
2. Repeat this again and say, ". . . greatness," thus completing two jumping jacks total.
3. Perform two more jumping jacks without saying anything, then resume repeating the mantra.
4. Repeat this pattern of two jumping jacks with the mantra and two without.
5. If you are modifying and not jumping, simply step your right leg out to the side as your arms come above your head and then bring your feet back together. Then step your left leg out and bring it back in. This will count as two jumping jacks.
6. Repeat the mantra 8 times.
7. The video will be particularly helpful on this one if you have any questions about the rhythm. You can view it here: www.erinstutland.com/gifts.

Move 2: Chair Pose Legs, Circle the Arms

Line 2: *I call in my success*
This mantra paired with the movement should make you feel like a super attractor! Sometimes we think success is just about taking action and moving toward *it*. But what if you started to see success also moving toward *you*? What if it was longing for you, the same way you were longing for it? Use this mantra and movement to call it in!

"I call in my success"

1. Bring your feet together and sit in a chair pose. Sit as low as you can.
2. Bring your arms to the position shown in the illustration, and circle your arms toward you as fast as you can. (This is different from the last time we did this movement, as now you are moving your arms toward yourself as opposed to away.)
3. Get those arms going, and whatever you do, don't stop. Find your own rhythm, and say, "I call in my success . . ."
4. You will be counting the number of times you say the mantra, but it doesn't matter how many circles of the arms you make. Repeat the mantra 16 times.

Move 1: Jumping Jack or Modified Jumping Jack

Line 3: *I am powerful*
This is a strong yet simple declarative statement. The truth is, you are powerful. Beyond measure. You have a voice, ideas, opinions, skills, and talent. You are unlike any other being on this planet. There are things you are able to do that no one else will ever do quite like you. This is your power. It's time to claim it and use it!

"I am powerful"

1. Start with your feet together, hands by your side. Jump your legs out to hips' distance apart as you bring your arms above your head, then jump your feet back together and bring your arms down. Say, "I am powerful."
2. Perform another jumping jack without saying anything.
3. You will alternate saying the mantra and doing the jumping jack and saying nothing.
4. If you are modifying and not jumping, simply step your right leg out to the side as your arms come

above your head and then bring your feet back together. Then step your left leg out and bring it back in. This will count as two jumping jacks.

5. Say the mantra 8 times. (You will have done 16 jumping jacks.)

Move 2: Chair Pose Legs, Circle the Arms

Line 4: *I attract the very best*

If you are someone who says things like, "Oh, I am never lucky," I want you to rethink that. I invite you to walk around saying and thinking that you are a person who attracts good things to themselves all day long. You attract brilliant people, great situations, and wonderful opportunities.

"I attract the very best"

1. Bring your feet together and sit in a chair pose. Sit as low as you can.
2. Bring your arms to the position shown in the illustration, and circle your arms toward you as fast as you can. (You are moving your arms toward yourself as opposed to away.)

3. Get those arms going, and whatever you do, don't stop. Find your own rhythm of this one, and say the mantra, "I attract the very best."
4. You will be counting the number of times you say the mantra, but it doesn't matter how many circles of the arms you make. Repeat the mantra 16 times.

Putting It All Together

Now you are going to put the *whole* thing together for 10 cycles. Alternate between Move 1 and Move 2. So it will flow like this:

Move 1: Jumping Jack or Modified Jumping Jack
Mantra: *I make space for greatness*
(Do 4 jumping jacks, only saying the mantra once. Then slowly lower to your chair pose for the next movement.)

Move 2: Chair Pose, Circle the Arms Toward You
Mantra: *I call in my success*
(Say the mantra once out loud while doing this and then think it one time to yourself as you continue to circle your arms. This will help with the rhythm.)

Move 1: Jumping Jack or Modified Jumping Jack
Mantra: *I am powerful*
(Do 4 jumping jacks and then bend into the chair pose for the next move.)

Move 2: Chair Pose, Circle the Arms Toward You
Mantra: *I attract the very best*
(Say the mantra one time, then think it a single time to yourself.)

You will repeat this whole cycle 10 times.

CELEBRATE!

Steve was preparing to marry his best friend and longtime love, Doug. He hadn't come out as gay until later in life, however, so he felt he'd spent most of his life hiding the most important parts of himself. One of the ways the hiding manifested was in extra weight, which is why Steve ended up as a participant on *Altar'd*. But he had a number of other goals he wanted to achieve that had nothing to do with the way he looked.

The weight was just a symptom of stress, fear, and low self-worth. But it was the first goal we'd tackle. During our first workout together, I could see doubt and hesitation on Steve's face. Standing on shaky legs, he could barely do a single lunge without holding on to something. It wasn't due to lack of physical strength, though; it was a shaky mind-set. With every exercise, it was as if he said to himself, "This is going to be too hard for me. I don't think I can do this."

But in spite of the shakes, Steve was determined. He wanted so much to step into a confident and calm version of himself. He wanted to give himself the best possible chance of happiness with Doug. So he committed to our plan. He showed up every day. He shook, he doubted, but he didn't give up. He even worked with a professional mountain biking teacher, who eventually had Steve going up and down some pretty steep hills for the first time in his life. It was thrilling to watch!

When it came time for his final weigh-in on the show, Steve walked into our meeting looking like a kid on Christmas morning. He was grinning from ear to ear and excited to find out what he'd accomplished during the 90 days of the program.

But when he stepped on the scale, he was about 15 pounds short of his goal. I was worried that he'd be disappointed, but Steve knew the numbers didn't matter. He was ecstatic because he'd accomplished so much. Even if he didn't reach his weight-loss goal, he *still* lost over 50 pounds! But most importantly, he felt more confident than he'd ever felt in his life. In 90 days' time—through pushing himself beyond his comfort zone physically, mentally, and emotionally—he had become a new person. It was a pleasure to give him a high five.

Steve reminded me of an important lesson—that we must celebrate our successes, even if we don't quite reach the absolute pinnacle we set our sights on.

Unfortunately, Steve is an unusual case among my clients. Most of them can't give themselves credit for what they've achieved if they don't manage to meet the goal they've set.

It's as if we believe we have to be relentless in order to ensure we never stop striving for more. But just like educators have discovered that positive reinforcement works better with students than negative feedback, the same holds true for the way we treat ourselves. It's encouragement that works, not criticism.

Rather than fall prey to the "never good enough" addiction, I say we need to celebrate every small achievement—and *that's* what will keep us motivated to strive for more.

As we talked about in Chapter 8, we can honor and appreciate where we are right in this moment and still keep moving forward without settling. The same can be said for celebrating. There's nothing wrong with marking more than just the big occasions like birthdays, weddings, graduations, anniversaries, and job promotions. We don't have to wait until we reach the top of Mt. Kilimanjaro before we deserve to be celebrated.

We give ourselves inspiration when we reward ourselves for a job well done, however small. A former teacher of mine used to say, "What we appreciate, appreciates." It's true. What we honor in our lives will grow and thrive. And as we celebrate, we *practice* the feeling of being accomplished. We can actually step into our rightful place as a successful person.

Celebration is much more than just an opportunity to feel good for a day. As we retrain our brain to stay focused on the positive outcome of our efforts, we become magnetic to more success.

I know of an actor who has worked steadily in the business for many years, yet he doesn't feel that he's "made it" because he isn't famous. He can't value his success because he feels he has to do more, be more, and have more. Nothing has ever been good enough. Meanwhile, other actors I know are envious of him because he's never had to wait tables or work in an office while trying to get acting work. It just goes to show that it's all in how we look at what we've achieved!

In this final chapter, we'll work on letting go of always striving for more so that we can celebrate the *right now*. You'll learn to celebrate yourself and appreciate every accomplishment. And I want to be there celebrating right along with you, if only in spirit! Here's our mantra:

What I appreciate, appreciates
I stay focused on my progress
Joy brings more joy
So I celebrate my success!

And again:

What I appreciate, appreciates
I stay focused on my progress
Joy brings more joy
So I celebrate my success!

Celebrating Changes Your Physiology and Strengthens Your Psychology

One of my best friends who had been searching for a soul mate for a long time finally met her person. All along, she wondered how she would meet someone since she didn't enjoy going out and being around a lot of people. She preferred cozy nights in, small groups, and low-key events. But she met someone anyway without having to go out in large groups. The fact that she didn't have to bend her personality to find love was a great example of how we're better off staying true to who we are.

After she announced her engagement, though, some of her close friends and I wanted to throw her an engagement party. But she resisted because the thought of spending a night out in a crowd of people made her nervous. But she reluctantly agreed, and we planned an event that suited her personality.

The evening brought together the people she loved most, and it further affirmed the inner work she had done that led her to finding her new love. It gave her a chance to acknowledge how far she'd come, and despite her reluctance, it turned out to be a very special night for her.

During the party, I could see my friend glowing from across the room. The next day, she confessed to me that she came to realize the importance of bringing everyone together to celebrate her success and happiness. It was a significant marker of her own personal milestone, and it helped her really drink in the idea that she had finally fallen in love, moving from wanting to having.

When we work for a long time to achieve a dream, we actually get comfortable in the longing phase. Then when we get what we want, it can be an adjustment. This is another reason why celebrating is so important. It helps us solidify our accomplishment and move the needle forward into a new way of being.

Then there's my client Katie. She always had a tendency to take care of others and put herself at the bottom of the list. One of her friends would call her last minute whenever she needed help with her dog, and Katie would run right over. Her family members relied on her to help them financially, yet it was rare that she treated herself to anything new or any kind of pampering.

But Katie recently made a commitment to move her body and do something good for herself every day by signing up for one of my weeklong movement challenges.

How'd she do? She completed it all without missing a day! Now, I know this may not sound like a big deal, but when you're used to putting yourself last, even taking five minutes for yourself can be a real challenge. But every day, she popped into our Facebook group and shared what she learned from that day's workout.

She had some revelations when she started pairing the movements with the mantras. She noticed the ways in which she was unkind to herself, and she confronted a few old beliefs about her body. She realized she hadn't allowed herself to acknowledge some of her desires that had been buried deep inside for a long time.

At the end of the week, Katie decided to celebrate her accomplishment by buying a nice warm vest that would allow her to continue her Soul Strolls during the winter. She had wanted the vest for a while, but she put it off, believing she didn't deserve it. Of course, she deserved it even before her accomplishment, but keeping her commitment to herself gave her the permission she needed to treat herself to an item that would help her continue with that commitment.

Katie's example is a smaller win than falling in love after years of trying to find someone, but it's important that we celebrate both the big milestones and the smaller achievements. When we don't celebrate our "smaller" wins, we train ourselves to think that what we do day-to-day isn't important or valuable. Then our life's moments start to blend together and become mundane. We stop giving 100 percent of ourselves *to* ourselves. The lack of celebration leads to a feeling of emptiness. We feel incomplete. What's the point, we think, if we're going to keep pushing ourselves, always believing that what we've done so far isn't enough?

Think about the last time you celebrated something in your life. Maybe it was an exciting new job or your wedding. I'm currently celebrating the arrival of my daughter and am looking forward to my book release party! But when was the last time you celebrated a seemingly small accomplishment like Katie's?

Moments like these release endorphins in our bodies, changing our physiology. They also give us the most incredible positive feelings, which strengthen our psychology. So why do we insist that we only commemorate the huge milestones? Why not have mini-celebrations for the small occasions and wins?

Did you just check a task off your to-do list that you've been putting off for a long time? Celebrate it! Did you say no to someone when you've been accustomed to crossing your own boundaries as a perpetual people pleaser? That sounds worthy of celebration to me!

Think about what it took to achieve that success. When we take the time to formally mark our accomplishments, we reinforce the behavior that helped us reach our goals.

Toward the end of my pregnancy, there were days when all I wanted to do was sit on the couch and eat ice cream. It got harder and harder to move, and the weight of the baby on my pelvis was almost unbearable. Yet I knew if I moved, I would have more energy and it would probably make for an easier delivery.

So I mustered up the courage to have a nice, long Soul Stroll with no definitive direction, set time frame, or destination. The only intention of my Soul Stroll was to connect with myself, my soul, God, the Universe, and life.

When I got home from my stroll, I did a little celebration dance to reinforce the behavior and mental push that got me out that door. I wanted to make sure I felt good about not just the walk, but the energy it took to get me there in the first place.

My client Pamela works in a restaurant part-time and always does little dances or high fives with others (or even just herself!) for the tiny, day-to-day wins. Whenever she gets a nice tip, she deposits the credit-card slip or cash into her drawer, kisses the paper, and says, "Thank you!"

I know you might feel silly celebrating your own successes if you don't have someone to celebrate with you. We're accustomed to partying with others at weddings, showers, and graduations. If we're enjoying a success, we feel as though there has to be someone else there to pat us on the back. But why isn't it enough to pat ourselves on the back? You can't count on someone else to acknowledge your achievements, especially the smaller ones along the way. But you can count on *yourself* to do that, and it's one of the most profound acts of self-love that I know. Remember this: you're an ocean, and sometimes you have to make your own waves. Don't wait for the waves to come to you.

If you're willing to celebrate yourself on your own, you'll generate a feeling of success in your body on a regular basis. Then success will become a way of being for you. Doesn't that sound wonderful?

I had a taste of this a few years ago when I first started making some money in my business. I was invited to a red-carpet premiere of a friend's movie. I wanted a beautiful dress for the occasion, but I was so accustomed to being a struggling artist that I rarely spent money on anything unnecessary. Nevertheless, I took myself shopping.

"I need something that will look smokin' on the red carpet," I told the salesperson. He pulled a few dresses off the rack and sent me into the dressing room. When I got there, I noticed the price tag on one of the dresses was $1,200! It was a plum-colored Herve Leger body-conscious dress that's made to hug your body in all the right places. Until that moment, I'd never even put anything that expensive on my body, let alone thought about buying it.

"You have to at least try it on," I told myself.

If you've ever tried on a very expensive dress, you understand why it costs so much. It was beautifully made, and the quality of the fabric was nothing short of scrumptious. When I walked out of the dressing room, the salesperson's jaw dropped. "You *have* to have this. How can you not buy this dress? It was made for you!"

I stared at myself in the mirror, and I had to admit he was right. It was perfect. I loved it.

Still, the conservative Midwestern girl in me couldn't wrap her head around spending so much money on a dress. "It's crazy," I heard her tell me in my head. "It's too much. Over the top. Inappropriate. *Too much* of a celebration!"

But for the first time in my life, I had enough money to buy the dress. I wouldn't have to go into debt for it, and I wanted to honor the hard work I'd put into my business. I had also recently ended a long relationship, and I was doing quite well, thank you very much. I really did have a lot to be proud of.

So—you guessed it—I bought the dress. It was a way that I could celebrate myself, even though it was definitely outside of my comfort zone. I didn't need anyone else to pat me on the back or to throw me a party. It was my own small, personal "proud of me" party. And you know what? The dress is such a classic that I still wear it and always get compliments when I do. The best part of wearing it, though, is that it brings back that feeling of celebration every time I put it on. It's a symbol and a reminder that celebrating ourselves is important, whether anyone else does it or not.

Now, I know buying a designer dress might not be for everyone, but you don't have to spend money at all to celebrate yourself. Years ago, when I finished creating the content for one of my online courses, I promised myself that once it was complete, I would take a day off, stay in bed, order my favorite Thai food, and binge on *Downton Abbey*. The idea of spending the entire day with characters I adored felt like as good a celebration as this girl could get, and it only cost me the price of my delivery food.

So just promise me that you'll love yourself enough to honor your achievements regularly. Okay? Do you promise?

Ideas for Celebration

Celebration is defined by its meaningfulness to you, not by its cost. Here are some cost-free ideas for commemorating your successes, but feel free to add your own ideas to the list.

No-Cost Ways to Celebrate

- Take a luxurious bath
- Take a Soul Stroll in a beautiful place—a nearby park or maybe an art museum
- Walk into a flower show or garden and smell the flowers
- Give yourself an hour to read your favorite book or listen to music you love
- Carve out a night to binge-watch that new TV show everyone's told you about

- Find a free concert, if possible, and enjoy it alone or with someone else
- Go into an expensive store and try on some of the clothes just for fun

Low-Cost Ways to Celebrate

- Get a massage or facial
- Buy a few of your favorite groceries and cook a beautiful meal
- Buy yourself flowers, perfume, or something else that's beautiful, thrills your senses, and makes you happy
- Go out with friends for drinks or dancing
- Go to a fancy hotel in your area for tea time
- See a movie at one of those theaters with cozy reclining seats and food that gets delivered to you
- Get a blowout, manicure, or pedicure

Journaling Exercise #17: Plan to Celebrate

Now that you have ideas, be on the lookout for reasons to celebrate during the next two weeks (and beyond), no matter how small. This will begin to make it a habit. Maybe you engaged in positive self-talk, stood up for yourself, or finally cleaned out that closet. Take 2 to 5 minutes to make note of your "small" successes, and make a plan for what you'll do to celebrate.

If you want to take a walk in a beautiful place, where will it be? If you want to try on clothes in an expensive store, which store will you choose? Write down what you'll do so that you're ready, and be sure to include when you will do it! It's easy to just think about it, but not actually do it. So be sure to write it down and get it in your schedule! So make sure you know when you're going to carve out the time. Whenever it's planned, you'll be saying no to something else and yes to celebrating yourself.

Be clear that this is what you're choosing to do with that time!

From now on, pay attention to the achievements you usually dismiss as unimportant. Recognize your growth step-by-step! You deserve it!

Before we move on, let's revisit our mantra:

What I appreciate, appreciates
I stay focused on my progress
Joy brings more joy
So I celebrate my success!

Celebrating with Others

While celebrating by ourselves can be sweet in its own way—giving us an opportunity to create that feeling of success from within—celebrating with other people is wonderful when we can do it.

When Steve, the man I talked about at the beginning of the chapter, got married to his soul mate and best friend, Doug, it was a beautiful occasion. I felt privileged to be there to watch the wedding of two people who were absolutely meant for each other.

The two of them had been very involved with the AIDS charity ride community, so their wedding was filled with people who loved them deeply. As they walked down the aisle together, there wasn't a dry eye in the crowd. It was a peak state of excitement that was contagious. Their joy filled everyone around them, and the happiness their guests felt for them was enough to fill the couple in turn. Everyone honored their success in finding and loving each other. (Yes, I believe finding love is a success.) It was a full circle of love and joy!

An elaborate party like a wedding is a special way to celebrate with friends, but even just marking a success with one friend can fill you with warmth and joy. It's another opportunity for a full-circle moment. When you can bring someone else into your celebration, do it. Do you have a best friend who can make a pact with you where you acknowledge each other's victories regularly so that you can each cultivate that successful feeling?

Of course, that means celebrating your *friends'* successes too. Now and then, however, when someone we know reaches a goal or is blessed in some way, we can still feel jealous and sad. Why can't that be us, we wonder?

When I first started running workshops, most of the attendees were performers who were constantly going on auditions for their dream roles. Since only one person can land those roles, my clients didn't get the job most of the time. Every so often, though, someone would score a role that made everyone else salivate.

Have you ever known someone who got the very thing you wanted? How did you feel? Was it hard to feel happy for this person? If so, you're hardly alone. Sometimes, when someone you know achieves something you've wanted for a long time, you may need to process your feelings about it. Don't feel that you have to instantly be happy for them. Allow yourself feelings of disappointment. Maybe their success makes you feel that time is of the essence or that you've missed the boat.

But after you've acknowledged and allowed your feelings, giving yourself some time to adjust to the news, I invite you to begin to look at it in another way. If someone close to you has manifested something you want, it's proof that what you want is possible to have! It might not come to you in exactly the same way or immediately, but if it can happen for them, why not you too?

If people around you are experiencing good fortune, it means the energy around you is ripe for you to do the same. You're in good company, attracting people who are thriving. It's important to switch your mind-set to "enoughness" in these moments. There's enough for both of you!

The next time you find yourself feeling a bit envious of someone else, remember that it means you're closer to your dream than you've ever been. Then, rather than go into the negative dumpers, try to step into their shoes and feel what they're feeling. Imagine that their success is yours. Go ahead and try that success on for size. Feel it in your bones, and live it "as if."

When the friend I mentioned earlier in the chapter called me to tell me about meeting "the one," her voice sounded giddy, but also calm and confident. I'd never heard her like that before.

At the time, my husband had been traveling quite a bit, and I was feeling frustrated and disconnected from him. I'll admit that there was a small part of me that felt jealous of my friend because I wasn't having similar feelings about my husband in that moment. But I like to practice feeling others' successes on a regular basis, so I let her words and emotions fill my soul. Within seconds, I felt her excitement as if it were my own.

I was taken right back to that precious, sweet time when my husband and I first fell in love. Through celebrating her in that moment, I was able to relive one of the best times in my life, almost instantly allowing myself to feel more connected to him. I took that energy forward when we got off the phone, and I called my husband to tell him I was planning a date night for us when he got back in town. I could hear the happiness in his voice, and I was so glad I allowed myself to celebrate her success in that way.

The bottom line, however, is that celebrating in whatever form—real, imaginary, alone, or with others—positions you as a winner and helps you attract more success. I don't know why we need an excuse to feel good or have a party, even if it's a party of one. What are you waiting for?

Meditation #8: Success in Your Bones

To do this meditation, you can record it yourself and play it back, or read through it and take it step-by-step.

1. Close your eyes, and begin to relax each part of your body, starting with your feet and legs and moving up to your torso, chest, arms, shoulders, neck, head, and face. You don't even have to know how to relax your body. Just tell yourself each part is relaxing.
2. Think of someone you know who has experienced a great success or celebration that made you feel envious. Imagine how this person felt—all the joy and satisfaction it brought them.

3. Imagine that you *are* this person. It's *your* success, *your* celebration, *your* joy, and *your* satisfaction. Can you allow yourself to feel it in your bones? It may be difficult at first, but experience it as fully as you can. What does it feel like to be standing in this place? Know that the more you try this, the better you'll become at taking on someone else's joy. Then you'll have this skill available to you whenever you need it.
4. Let go of your friend's feelings, and let's recall your own. Think of the time when you experienced your most significant success or celebration. Maybe you got your dream job, got married, had a baby, or even was praised for a job well done. Whatever it is, remember it in as much detail as you can. What were the sights, sounds, smells, tastes, and textures? How did you feel?
5. Take a few minutes to bring back those feelings as intensely as you can. Revisit the joy and happiness you felt. Again, feel it in your bones, and sink deeply into it. Allow yourself to bask in those feelings as long as you want.
6. Know that you can go back to these feelings whenever you wish. Even if you're going through a very difficult time, remembering a more joyful time can take the edge off your current pain. You can even choose one image or a word that reminds you of that joyful time and use it as a trigger the next time you want to recall the feelings. All you have to do is think of that image or say that word in your mind, and you'll be there.
7. Open your eyes when you're ready, but don't let go of the joyful feelings. Let's put them to good use while you work out with your mantra!

MANTRA IN MOTION #9

This workout is your celebration of how far you've come through the process of this book. It's important to remember that when we appreciate all we have and all we are, it creates room for those things to appreciate or grow. As you continue to apply what you've learned in your life, I invite you to come back to this workout every time you want to move the needle a little further in the direction you want to go.

I'm so proud of you, and I'm celebrating you as I write this, knowing that if you're reading these words, you've taken several very real steps toward your dreams. Bravo!

Your Celebration Mantra

What I appreciate, appreciates
I stay focused on my progress
Joy brings more joy
So I celebrate my success!

Move 1: Squat with Arm Extension

Line 1: *What I appreciate, appreciates*
I want you to think of all the amazing things in your life right now—big and small. Maybe you have a super cozy bed. Maybe you have great friends. Maybe you love the shoes on your feet. Maybe you have a partner that you love. All of these things, and more, are important to appreciate. As we appreciate them, the good things tend to grow and multiply. You are going to want some music for this movement sequence for sure!

"What I appreciate, appreciates"

1. Start facing forward at 12 o'clock with your feet together. Step your right leg back to 4 or 5 o'clock so that you are on a slight diagonal. Step back to a squat, with your right hand on your heart and your left arm extended out in front of you.
2. Bring your left index finger and thumb together, with your left arm extended out in front of you. Allow your eyes to focus on the circle that you make with your hands. Try to envision all the things you appreciate while looking through the hole.
3. As you step back to the squat, say, "What I appreciate . . ." Then step your foot back in.
4. Step back on your left leg, doing the same thing with your arms but on the opposite side. As you step back on your left leg, say, ". . . appreciates." Then step your foot back in.
5. Each squat is one rep. You will repeat the mantra 16 times, effectively doing 8 squats on each side.

Move 2: Clap and Dance

Line 2: *I stay focused on my progress*
What we focus on grows and expands. Remember that this is not about perfection, but about progress. When you can stay tuned in to the progress you are making, you feel better and are naturally more encouraged. So let's stay focused on how far you have come! This movement and mantra are going to require that you have a little fun. Are you ready for that?

"I stay focused on my progress"

1. You are going to make this movement your own, so make sure that music is pumpin'!
2. Clap your hands as fast as you can. Yes, that's right, clap your hands like you are celebrating your life! You can dance around, do a step touch, skip, or jump up and down. Whatever you do, I want you to focus on getting the energy up in your mind and your body.
3. As you clap it out, say, "I stay focused on my progress!"
4. Repeat this mantra with enthusiasm 16 times.

Move 1: Squat with Arm Extension

Line 3: *Joy brings more joy*
Some of us struggle to let ourselves really feel joy in our hearts because we are afraid it won't last. The truth is, feelings ebb and flow, but when we allow ourselves to feel joy, we get more comfortable with this feeling and it allows us to attract more of it. Stay focused on the joy you have as a way to call in more!

"Joy brings more joy"

1. Start facing forward at 12 o'clock with your feet together. Step your right leg back to 4 or 5 o'clock so that you are on a slight diagonal. Step back to a squat, with your right hand on your heart and your left arm extended out in front of you.
2. Bring your left index finger and thumb together, with your left arm extended out in front of you. Allow your eyes to focus on the circle you make with your hands. This is your progress.
3. As you step back to the squat, say, "Joy . . ." Then step your feet together.

4. Step back on your left leg, doing the opposite of the previous step with your arms, and say, ". . . brings more joy." Then step your feet back together.
5. You will say the mantra 16 times, so you will end up doing 8 squats per side.

Move 2: Clap and Dance

Line 4: *So I celebrate my success*
All right, friend, this is your big finish! I want you to leave it all on the floor, saving nothing. I want you to clap to celebrate every success you have ever had and every success that is coming your way. Don't be shy here. Don't be stingy! It's time to celebrate all you are and all you are becoming!

"So I celebrate my success"

1. You are going to make this movement your own, so keep the music going!
2. Clap your hands as fast as you can. See if you can generate feelings of joy and love as you do this. You can dance around, do a step touch, skip, or jump

up and down. Get that energy up in your mind and your body.

3. As you clap it out, say, "So I celebrate my success!"
4. Repeat this mantra with joy 16 times.

Putting It All Together

Now you are going to put the *whole* thing together for 10 cycles. Alternate between Move 1 and Move 2. So it will flow like this:

Move 1: Squat with Arm Extension
Mantra: *What I appreciate, appreciates*
(After you do this, get ready to move and shake!)

Move 2: Clap and Dance
Mantra: *I stay focused on my progress*
(Let yourself have some fun with this one; don't worry how long or short you go!)

Move 1: Squat with Arm Extension
Mantra: *Joy brings more joy*
(Get ready to celebrate!)

Move 2: Clap and Dance
Mantra: *So I celebrate my success*
(Let yourself go on this; there are no rules in this celebration!)
Repeat this whole cycle 10 times, increasing in energy and enthusiasm as you go!

YOUR 14-DAY PLAN TO CREATE YOUR SWEET LIFE

Most of us are ready to change. It's just that we feel we don't know *how* to do it.

We know *why*: we want to make the life of our dreams a reality. But how do we start? With so many programs, methods, and options, it's easy to get pulled in a million different directions and get stuck.

That's why I created this 14-Day Plan—to take the guesswork out of feeling wonderful in your body and life. This program will allow you to put the movement and mantras you've learned in the book into practice each day for two weeks. Each day, I'll suggest a movement sequence from one of our chapters, and I'll give you a short daily activity to boost your creativity and keep you feeling inspired. You'll build from one day to the next toward creating what you want in your life.

I purposely kept the 14-Day Plan simple and easy to follow. I wanted to show you that small steps taken over just a two-week period can lead to big changes. Remember that Martin Luther King, Jr., reminds us to take the first step even if we can't see the whole staircase.

Between the movement and the short activity, each day's assignment should take you no longer than 10 minutes. As you get ready to perform the moves and mantras, I highly recommend pulling up the web page with videos of several of the mantra and movement sequences. You'll then be moving with a friend (me!), and I'll encourage you through each move. You can find it here: www.erinstutland.com/gifts.

If you've flipped to this portion of the book without going through all the chapters, that's absolutely okay. As a coach who has worked with people in person and online, I know that some of us learn best through starting with a physical experience, while others learn best when they first engage their minds and understand the process intellectually.

If you're someone who prefers to dive right into the physical experience, however, please go back at some point and do the journaling exercises and meditations within the book that resonate with the issues you're facing in your life. They're the groundwork that will solidify the work you do in this 14-Day Plan, but this plan is *no substitute* for that groundwork.

For those of you who have read through most of the book first, the 14-Day Plan will keep your momentum in motion with daily touch points that build on what you've already discovered. By revisiting the movements and mantras, you'll reconnect with the ideas that you generated as you moved through the book.

Either way, I want you to continue to make this book your own and use it in the way that best works for you. That said, I strongly suggest that you read the plan for each day in the morning so that you can set your intention for the day. You could also read it the night before, but I suggest reading it again in the morning. When you've finished the 14-Day Plan, you can go back and start from Day 1 again, or you can use the plan to design your own new plan based on the chapters and mantras within the book.

If you are looking for more support, encouragement, and accountability, I have listed several ways to get that in the Resources section at the end of the book.

As you start the program, you might find yourself thinking, *This is silly and won't work.* I invite you to turn off the part of your brain that wants to pass judgment and tap into the parts of your soul that crave lightness, ease, and fun.

Are you ready? Let's go!

Day 1

Your Day 1 Movement with Mantra

Today, you'll do the movement sequence from Chapter 2 (page 38). It's so important to set intentions based on how you want to *feel*. I'm guessing you *don't* want to feel exhausted, stuck, sad, or like you don't measure up in some way. So we're going to get crystal clear on how you *do* want to feel. You'll claim a renewed sense of purpose for your life and discover your own unstoppable power to go for and get what you want.

Here's the mantra:

I let my desire guide me
I do what feels right
I stay true to my vision
I keep love in sight!

Your Day 1 Activity

Do you ever catch yourself saying, "This is too hard" or "I can't do it" or "The problem is . . ."? Today, we're going to actively challenge that urge by *flipping your mental script*. Count how many times you say "I can't" or some form of it throughout the day. How many times do you stop yourself from doing something because you don't think you're capable? At the end of the day, tally them up.

Whatever your number, see if you can lower it by one tomorrow. If your number was eight, make it seven tomorrow. Keep lowering the number day after day until you've eliminated this way of thinking entirely. You're training your brain to stay focused on what you *can* do, which is much more than you believe!

Day 2

Your Day 2 Movement with Mantra

Today, let's repeat the movement sequence from Chapter 2 (page 38). We're going to play a little game. It's important that you get very clear on not only how you want to *feel,* but also what you want to manifest in your life. Maybe you have a vision for the next year of your life. Or maybe a year is too much. You can even focus on the week ahead.

If you could have anything happen in your life, or you had the ability to attract something wonderful and special, what would it be? Can you visualize it? Can you imagine it happening? I invite you to keep this vision in mind as you perform today's workout.

If doubt creeps in, don't judge it. We're working on reprogramming your script. It may take some time, so complete the movement and mantra anyway.

Here's your mantra again. Yes, it's the same as yesterday's in order to reinforce its power in your mind, heart, and body:

I let my desire guide me
I do what feels right
I stay true to my vision
I keep love in sight!

Your Day 2 Activity

Today, you brought to mind something specific that you want to see happen in your life. Hopefully, you are able to visualize and feel it. Tonight, I invite you to take a few minutes to visualize your desire coming true with ease.

Once you're comfortable in bed, take a few deep breaths and scan your body. Notice if there are tight spots anywhere. If so, just send your breath into those areas on each exhale. When you feel relaxed, bring your desire to mind. Practice "as if" it's already true. Come up with as many details as you can until you slowly drift off to sleep.

Day 3

Your Day 3 Movement with Mantra

Today, I invite you to use the movement sequence from Chapter 3 (page 62). So much of our inability to get what we want is due to our own resistance. When we take a little time to tune in to the present moment and allow life to flow, we find there's more ease to our days. Here's your mantra:

I am tuned in
I step into the flow
I have all that I need
The rest I let go!

Your Day 3 Activity

Are there any ways you are making it harder for Life and the Universe to support you and bring you all you want? Are you sending any mixed messages or telling any old stories that might confuse the miracles headed your way?

Richard Branson has a nickname among employees at his Virgin empire—"Doctor Yes." He got that nickname because of how often he says yes to Life. It can make all the difference in the world to say that one word to whatever sounds fun or exciting.

Today, I ask you to practice saying yes to everything you can. (That might mean saying no to habits like taking care of others rather than yourself.) It will likely feel challenging, but tell yourself for now that it's just for today. Give it a try. Just say, "Yes, yes, yes!"

DAY 4

Your Day 4 Movement with Mantra

Today, we dive into your beliefs. Remember: beliefs that hold you back can be changed, and new beliefs can be created. You are not stuck. Repeat that with me: "I am not stuck!" What beliefs do you need to let go of, and what new ones do you need to call in? Bring those to mind as you perform the movement and mantras. *Believe* in your ability to change your beliefs.

This movement sequence is from Chapter 4 (page 80). Here's your mantra:

I let go of the old
I'm creating something new
I choose my beliefs
It's easy to do!

Your Day 4 Activity

What have you told yourself is difficult? Maybe it's exercising regularly, finding a mate, or making more money. Do you have a mental script that says, "That's really going to be hard" or "That's too difficult" or "I could never do that"? The belief that our dreams will be hard to accomplish are ingrained in us from childhood. Maybe a parent taught you to believe that life in general is tough.

So today, I want you to explore the concept of ease. One way to do that is to simply nod your head yes while saying, "I've got this; it's easy." I like to do this several times throughout the day. You can do it in response to a stressful thought, or just try it right now to see how the simple motion feels in your body as you say, "I've got this; it's easy." Don't worry if you don't believe it completely yet. Nod and say it anyway! That simple head gesture will give your body the message and begin to change how you feel.

Day 5

Your Day 5 Movement with Mantra

Beliefs can take some time to change, especially if you've carried them for a long time, so this sequence bears repeating. I want you to truly get that you can create a new way of thinking, being, and feeling. If you had any doubts yesterday about your ability to choose your beliefs, let today be an opportunity to work those out a little more. And if you were feeling on fire with it yesterday, you might want to choose a new belief to unstick today! Again, here's your mantra (see page 80 for the movement sequence instructions):

I let go of the old
I'm creating something new
I choose my beliefs
It's easy to do!

Your Day 5 Activity

Most of us have a very hard time receiving compliments, let alone giving them to ourselves. We focus on what we didn't do and haven't done so that we forget to love ourselves for all we *have* done. You deserve to be showered in love. Yes, you do—trust me!

So today, give yourself five compliments. That's right—I said *five*! For example: "It's great that I got through all my emails, even when I felt like shutting down." "I'm awesome because I went for a walk this morning and got in my steps." "I'm treating my body well because I chose a healthy lunch when I had other options." "I'm making real progress because I didn't freak out when my kids started screaming." It can be anything; just take the time to acknowledge it.

Why spend your precious time in life being hard on yourself? Instead, spend it loving yourself with the kind of forgiveness and encouragement that you give other people. Amazing things will start to happen!

Day 6

Your Day 6 Movement with Mantra

Today is all about cultivating courage! I'd like you to do the movement sequence from Chapter 6 (page 125) *twice*. Are you willing? (It will just take 10 minutes!)

Why twice? It's a big day because I'm going to ask you to practice stepping out of your comfort zone. I want you to truly embody what it feels like to be courageous. You may want to do this only once, but let's find out what happens when you sustain that feeling of courage for 10 whole minutes (even if it makes you a little uncomfortable). Here's your mantra:

It's my time
Today's the day
I will feel the fear
And I will do it anyway!

Your Day 6 Activity

Little acts of courage are performed every day, yet they often go unnoticed. Today, keep a log of all your victories. Yes, even the small ones like "got out of bed," especially if, like me, you aren't an early riser!

Make sure you write down at least three accomplishments today. Nothing is too inconsequential: "I went to the gym even though I didn't want to." "I paid all my bills." "I turned down a slice of my mother's famous chocolate cake."

You might want to make this a daily practice, though, because if you're feeling down, you can go back and read your log for an instant pick-me-up. It only has to amount to a few sentences a day, but you'll be amazed six months from now when you look back and see how many successes you've racked up!

Day 7

Your Day 7 Movement with Mantra

Today is all about taking *action*! Are you ready to move forward in your life? Ideas without action are just dreams, and while dreaming is important, dreams only live in our minds. I want you to take the ideas and dreams in your mind and turn them into something tangible that you can touch, feel, talk about, and be proud of! Choose a specific dream you want to fulfill, and think about it as you work out and chant your mantra. Visualize it, feel it, and make it happen!

Today, you'll do the movement sequence from Chapter 5 (page 103). Here's your mantra:

I am taking action
I have love in my soul
No worries, no regrets
I am ready to go!

Your Day 7 Activity

How many times have you heard the phrase "Good things come to those who wait"? I respectfully disagree. I believe good things come to those who *act*, and *great* things come to those who act from a place of inspiration and confidence.

Today is all about kicking your fears to the curb and taking action. If that sounds daunting, I want you to stop right now—yes, right now!—and think of one task you've been putting off. Write it down. If it needs to be broken down into smaller steps, go ahead and do that now. For example, if I've been putting off rewriting my résumé, I might break that down into four smaller steps: (1) review my old résumé, (2) write down what I can add to the résumé since it was last written, (3) look for ways to change the résumé to reflect how I want to position myself in the marketplace now, and (4) have my friend Sonia review it. Then don't forget to write next to each task how long it will take you to finish it.

Next, pick one of them, set your timer, and do at least the first step toward that goal *right now*. Don't wait another moment!

Day 8

Your Day 8 Movement with Mantra

If you don't take action on your dreams and ideas, you're simply a dreamer. Taking regular action, even when you don't feel like it or even when you feel afraid, is a skill that can be strengthened over time.

Because taking action is such an important part of getting what you want, we're going to repeat the movement sequence from Chapter 5 (page 103). If you felt proud yesterday after you took action, I want to prove to you that it wasn't just a fluke. That pride was a result of stepping up and moving forward. Again, here's your mantra:

I am taking action
I have love in my soul
No worries, no regrets
I am ready to go!

Your Day 8 Activity

Revisit your list of actions from yesterday. Either pick another task from yesterday's list, or pick another action you have been putting off. Break it down into smaller steps if need be, and write down how much time each step will take you. Then take those actions! As Gandhi once said, "Just do it." (Just kidding. That wasn't Gandhi. It's Nike. You catch my drift.) *Act!*

Day 9

Your Day 9 Movement with Mantra

Today, we'll focus on honoring the courage you already have as a way of encouraging even more. If you have made it to Day 9, it means you've already had the courage to get up out of your seat and move your body eight days in a row while saying mantras out loud.

Don't take that accomplishment lightly. It takes courage! As a reminder, here is today's mantra (see page 125 for the movement sequence instructions):

It's my time
Today's the day
I will feel the fear
And I will do it anyway!

Your Day 9 Activity

Today, I want you to think of three people who are courageous. That doesn't mean they're doing anything harrowing. Maybe you witnessed someone stick up for someone else who wasn't treated well. Maybe you have a friend who had the courage to leave a relationship that wasn't working. Recently, a friend of mine got asked to speak at a conference and had the courage to ask for more money than what they were offering. It was out of his comfort zone, but he got the additional funds because he asked. Or perhaps you read an article about a person who overcame a fear or obstacle.

Every day, people we know are courageous. Extra bonus points if you reach out to that person to tell them how much you admire their bravery.

Day 10

Your Day 10 Movement with Mantra

Today, we're focused on gathering your support system so that you feel bolstered by the people and situations in your life, as opposed to held back by any of them. I'd like you to revisit the movement sequence from Chapter 7 (page 150). Here's your mantra:

I release my doubts
It's all working out
Support is all around
I am breaking new ground!

Your Day 10 Activity

Hopefully, by now you feel as though you're always being supported by a benevolent and loving Universe. But who else could we add to your list of cheerleaders? My guess is that there are people in your life who want to see you succeed. It could even be people you don't frequently see or talk to. Think about people in your past as well. Was there a teacher who cheered you on? Was there a friend from your childhood who always thought you walked on water?

Give yourself seven minutes to write a list of every single person who ever rooted for you. Whoever comes to mind is perfect. It doesn't have to be a long list—just enough to remind yourself that you aren't alone.

Day 11

Your Day 11 Movement with Mantra

Today, let's repeat the movement sequence from Chapter 7 (page 150). We'll focus on how *you* can support yourself. Before you start today's workout, take a moment to thank yourself for coming this far. Place your hands over your heart in a gesture of gratitude. You've already been committed to this plan for 10 days. That has required a lot of courage and dedication. It also shows you can support yourself!

Here's your mantra:

I release my doubts
It's all working out
Support is all around
I am breaking new ground!

Your Day 11 Activity

Write yourself a thank-you note! Because you've shown up for yourself throughout this book and plan, you've proven that when you take it one day at a time, one step at a time, you can succeed and create change in your life. What is one change you've noticed so far? Include that in your thank-you note to yourself. It might just be feeling a little more positive or confident, but that isn't small! It's a big step in the right direction.

Write your thank-you note in your journal, send it to yourself in an email, or bust out the old-fashioned, handwritten thank-you cards, and snail mail it to yourself for bonus points.

DAY 12

Your Day 12 Movement with Mantra

Today, we'll do the movement sequence from Chapter 8 (page 168). This is one of my favorites but often one of the hardest for us to do. It's difficult to accept that life is unfolding exactly as it should. But when we open our minds to the idea that if we take inspired action, what we need will show up at the perfect time, and our lives suddenly get easier.

Remember this as you perform today's workout. Here's your mantra:

What is for me cannot pass me
What is meant for me will arrive
Perfect people, perfect choices
Perfect opportunities in perfect time!

Your Day 12 Activity

I love to read inspiring passages from books and meditate on them as I let them sink into my mind and heart. As you begin your day, read the following, and let it fill you up with the belief that all is well today and every day. Then set an alarm on your phone at lunch time, and before you go to bed, reread it:

"One day, you'll awake to discover your life is all you wanted and hoped it would be. Oh, you'll not find everything just the way your head said you wanted it. It might not be the way you planned. But you'll awaken to your dreams—your dreams of joy, love and peace. Your dream of freedom. You'll see beyond the illusions, you'll transcend your old limiting beliefs. You'll wake up and notice that your past is just as it needed to be. You'll see where you are today is good. You'll notice that you laugh a lot, cry a lot, smile a lot. You'll look at tomorrow with peace, faith and hope—knowing that while you cannot control some of what life does, you have possibilities and powers in any circumstance life might bring. The struggle you have lived with for so many years, the struggle in your heart has disappeared. You're secure and at peace with yourself and your place in this world. One day, you'll awaken to your heart's contentment. Let that day be today." — Melody Beattie, Journey to the Heart: Daily Meditations on the Path to Freeing Your Soul

Day 13

Your Day 13 Movement with Mantra

In order to live the life you want, you've learned that you need to make room for greatness. Throughout these last several days, you've done a tremendous amount of inner and outer work. You've looked at your beliefs, cultivated courage, taken action upon action, and let it all go.

Now it's time to call in your success! You'll use the movement sequence from Chapter 9 (page 188). Here's your mantra:

I make space for greatness
I call in my success
I am powerful
I attract the very best!

Your Day 13 Activity

In addition to the moves and mantra, let's head outside for a Soul Stroll. As you may recall, a Soul Stroll is a walk with no particular destination. Instead, it's simply to connect with yourself and your greatness. It is a perfect activity as we near the end of this program. Let your mind relax as you put one foot in front of the other, and feel the fresh air on your skin as you make room for greatness with joy and ease!

For a little extra oomph, you can come to this link: www.erinstutland.com/free-soul-stroll to download a free starter Soul Stroll playlist that I created. You'll recognize some of the mantras.

Day 14

Your Day 14 Movement with Mantra

You did it! I'm so proud of you. You got through two weeks of movement and mantras while focusing on what you want in your life! If any part of you is thinking, *But I didn't do it perfectly,* I want you to remember what we discussed about perfection. Perfection means completing—nothing more. If you're about to finish Day 14, it means you have completed this plan, which means you have done it perfectly!

Hopefully, you're feeling empowered and connected to the best parts of yourself. So now it's time to celebrate! Here's your mantra (see page 208 for the movement sequence instructions):

What I appreciate, appreciates
I stay focused on my progress
Joy brings more joy
So I celebrate my success!

Your Day 14 Activity

Today, I want you to track down your favorite quote—words that remind you of who you are, who you want to become, or why you do what you do. It might even be one of the mantras from this book that you want to remember on a regular basis. Then I want you to commit it to memory. This quote or mantra is going to be your true north for as long as you need it—the next several weeks, months, or maybe even years. They are words you will live by and a lesson you'll want to pass on to your friends and family. I don't think there's anything more powerful than sharing encouraging and inspiring words with the people you love.

Using an app on your phone, make an infographic of your quote. I also invite you to write it down so that you see it regularly.

If you haven't yet come over to say "hello" on any of my social media channels, please find me on Facebook at https://www.facebook.com/EStutland/ or Instagram @erin.stutland. I would love to hear from you. Share the quote or mantra you chose, and tell me why it's important to you. What have you learned over these past 14 days or during the course of reading the book? What has shifted for you? Do you feel different in your body? Is your mind clearer?

I also invite you to tell a friend about your journey so far. This will help solidify what you've learned while also inspiring your friend to make positive changes. The work you've done using the exercises, meditations, movements, and mantras is powerful. Don't minimize the impact that mindful movement can have when paired with your desires, your courage, and your creative ideas to design a life you love!

What happens next? Well, first, I hope you'll take a moment to celebrate yourself! Then I invite you to head to the Resources (page 239), where I've created a bunch of ways for you to keep this good energy going, as well as ways for us to stay in touch.

My friend, if you like how you are feeling, we're just getting started!

FINAL WORDS: MY WISH FOR YOU

My hope is that a new way of thinking is taking root in your mind, your body, and your spirit. That you're beginning to truly connect with the power you have to make your life your very own masterpiece in which you co-design the moments, days, weeks, and years into what you most desire.

I purposely chose the word *co-design* because we never do anything alone. We're all a part of a magical network of people, opportunities, and experiences that, put together, is much bigger than we are as individuals. Life constantly shows us this in the glory of a sunset, the waves of the ocean, or even in the small, surprising text message from an old friend. I invite you to stay in a state of awe, wonder, curiosity, and interest. I invite you to ask the ego, fear, stubbornness, stinginess, and feeling of lack to move aside and *allow life* to truly show its magnificence to you on a daily basis.

Of course, you must participate. Buy the plane ticket. Go on the date. Take yourself to the gym. Put on your flip-flops, and walk to the ocean to watch that beautiful sunset or sunrise. Take action and experiment. It will build your confidence. Showing up again and again will help you discover your likes and dislikes, refine your thoughts, and align with what you love rather than with what you fear. The confidence you gain will give you the courage to allow and accept the beauty that life wants to give you.

More than anything, I want you to know that you can do it. You are not stuck! You have the power. You have the courage. You have the strength. You have the ability. You can tune in. You can step into the flow. You have all that you need, and the rest, my sweet friend, you can let go.

This is truly your time. Yours for the taking. Become the leader you have been waiting for. You don't need anyone else to give you permission to do what you long to do. Step forward every day like a new babe out of the womb. As the amazing Louise Hay said, "Your power is always in the present moment." Let yourself live it!

I wish you a clear mind, a loving heart, and a strong body to carry you forward toward your dreams.

Love,
Erin

RESOURCES

None of us goes at this alone! I would love to help you keep your Mantras in Motion! Here are a few great options for you to continue to create movement in your body and movement in your life.

Stay Connected

Take the **What's Your Mantra Quiz** to get a FREE personalized mantra and movement for your life right now. The assessment will help you understand what you need most to get physically and mentally focused and ready to manifest what you want: erinstutland.com/mantra-quiz.

Sign up for my weekly(ish) **#Mantrasinmotion newsletter** where I share my behind-the-scenes updates—along with a curated list of new mantras, helpful articles, podcasts, and manifesting tools: erinstutland.com/list.

You can also follow me on Instagram @erin.stutland for weekly mantras and other inspirational posts.

Keep Moving

Join the Say it, Sweat it, Get it FREE Challenge: It doesn't take going to extremes to get a body and a life you love. If you enjoyed the movements from this book, you will love this week-long challenge where, together, we will do short, easy-to-do workouts that will lift you up—mind, body and spirit. Join the Challenge here: erinstutland.com/free-challenge.

Sign up for a **FREE Soul Stroll Playlist** to help you walk, run, and simply move your way to feeling inspired! erinstutland .com/free-soul-stroll

Go Deeper

Shrink Session Program: Work out with me from anywhere in the world with an international and supportive community. The program includes a variety of workouts, meditations, and coachings to help you create both a body and life you love. Learn more: erinstutland.com/shrink-session.

Soul Strolls: I have created a series of affordable Soul Stroll packages that come with a soundtrack, workout, meditation, and 10-day program. They all have unique mantras, music, and coaching to help move you mentally, physically, and spiritually! Learn more: erinstutland.com/soul-stroll.

Coaching, Teacher Training, and Live Classes and Workshops: If you're interested in accelerating your goals, wanting to bring this method to your local fitness/yoga studio or gym or wanting to energize your workplace, see the full list of ways we can work together in person. Learn more: erinstutland.com/work-with-me.

INDEX

D

E

F

G

H

I

J

K

L

M

N

O

P

Q

R

S

T

U

V

W

Y

ACKNOWLEDGMENTS

This book took full shape when I was pregnant with my daughter, Kwynn. Not only that, but shortly after I started writing, we got picked up for a second season of *Altar'd*. Growing a human, shooting a TV show, and writing a book all at once is no small feat. There are many people I could not do it without.

To Lance, my husband and my love, rerunning into you at a New York City gym couldn't have been more perfect. You saw me in my glory—teaching, dancing, and sharing my passion. You have supported all of it ever since. I am the luckiest girl in the world to have you by my side.

To Kwynn, thank you for being such an easy, sweet baby while I finished the book edits. More importantly, thank you for giving me the incredible gift of motherhood. The overflowing joy you bring is indescribable. I promise to continue to make you proud.

To Mom and Dad, this book is only one of the many things I have created because you believed in me and supported me unconditionally. You are the foundation for which my whole beautiful life rests. Thank you.

To my brother, Brian, and sister-in-law, Donnie, thank you for your support from the very beginning when I started my business. Everything I learned, thanks to your help, has given me the ability to do what I love and help others. I am so grateful.

Book Team and Support Circle:

Wendy Sherman, my agent, for believing in this vision and bringing your smart, caring, nurturing self to every conversation and meeting.

Melanie Votaw, your ability to help crystalize ideas and make them better is your superpower. I am grateful to be on the receiving end of it.

Lisa Cheng, my editor at the Hay House family, for making this book the best it could be and helping to shape it to perfection.

Patty Gift and Reid Tracy, for inviting me to be a part of this incredible community of inspiring and gifted authors. I am so humbled.

Laura Baran, for the whimsical illustrations. What a gift to get to work with a dear friend.

Mary Carol Fitzgerald, for the beautiful cover image.

Lynn Crymble, for keeping the business running and keeping me sane during such a whirlwind of a time.

Samantha Chagollan, for all the extra edit love.

My Tribe of Women: There is power when women gather, share ideas, support one another, cheer each other on, and laugh. Laughter is a key. I hope my daughter is as lucky as I am to have such an outstanding community of emotionally intelligent, sensitive, bold, go-getting women. You all are changing the world for the better. I love you.

Shonda Howard, Jessica Ortner, Heather Pierce Giannone, Marni Helfand, Melissa Goldenberg, Julie-Anne Lee Kinney, Alex Jameison, Nicole Jardim, Rebekkah Borucki, Danielle Diamond, Kris Carr, Robyn Youkilis, Jeannine Yoeder, Jenn Raccipi, Tracy Campoli, Karie Grey, Sarah Dade, Kate Northrup, Laura Garnett, CC Hirsch, Jenny Blakely, Amy Zemnick, and Beri Cohen.

ABOUT THE AUTHOR

Erin Stutland is a mind-body wellness and fitness expert, and the host and coach of the weight-loss transformation TV show *Altar'd* on Z Living. Erin has guided thousands of people through her mind-body fitness programs, including her signature "Shrink Session" workout and "Soul Strolls."

Erin has appeared on the *Rachael Ray Show*, Fox News, and KTLA, and in *Glamour, Shape, Yoga Journal, Real Simple, Reader's Digest, U.S. News & World Report, Weight Watchers Magazine*, and more. She has collaborated with thought leaders, such as *New York Times* best-selling authors Kris Carr and Jessica Ortner, helping to bring healthy movement to the masses. She is AFAA certified (and has training certs in several fitness programs) and holds a BFA in dance and kinesiology.

She currently lives in Brooklyn, New York, with her husband, Lance, and daughter, Kwynn.

You can visit her online at erinstutland.com.

Follow Erin on Instagram @erin.stutland and on Facebook: https://www.facebook.com/erin.stutland.

Hay House Titles of Related Interest

YOU CAN HEAL YOUR LIFE, the movie,
starring Louise Hay & Friends
(available as a 1-DVD program, an expanded 2-DVD set,
and an online streaming video)
Learn more at www.hayhouse.com/louise-movie

THE SHIFT, the movie,
starring Dr. Wayne W. Dyer
(available as a 1-DVD program, an expanded 2-DVD set,
and an online streaming video)
Learn more at www.hayhouse.com/the-shift-movie

***

OWN YOUR GLOW: A Soulful Guide to Luminous Living and Crowning the Queen Within, by Latham Thomas

THE POWER OF ATTENTION: Awaken to Love and Its Unlimited Potential with Meditation, by Sarah McLean

THE UNIVERSE HAS YOUR BACK: Transform Fear to Faith, by Gabrielle Bernstein

YOU HAVE 4 MINUTES TO CHANGE YOUR LIFE: Simple 4-Minute Meditations for Inspiration, Transformation, and True Bliss, by Rebekah Borucki

All of the above are available at your local bookstore,
or may be ordered by contacting Hay House (see next page).

***

We hope you enjoyed this Hay House book. If you'd like to receive our online catalog featuring additional information on Hay House books and products, or if you'd like to find out more about the Hay Foundation, please contact:

Hay House, Inc., P.O. Box 5100, Carlsbad, CA 92018-5100
(760) 431-7695 or (800) 654-5126
(760) 431-6948 (fax) or (800) 650-5115 (fax)
www.hayhouse.com® • www.hayfoundation.org

Published in Australia by:
Hay House Australia Pty. Ltd., 18/36 Ralph St., Alexandria NSW 2015
Phone: 612-9669-4299 • *Fax:* 612-9669-4144 • www.hayhouse.com.au

Published in the United Kingdom by:
Hay House UK, Ltd., Astley House, 33 Notting Hill Gate, London W11 3JQ
Phone: 44-20-3675-2450 • *Fax:* 44-20-3675-2451 • www.hayhouse.co.uk

Published in India by: Hay House Publishers India,
Muskaan Complex, Plot No. 3, B-2, Vasant Kunj, New Delhi 110 070
Phone: 91-11-4176-1620 • *Fax:* 91-11-4176-1630 • www.hayhouse.co.in

---